The ATARI Experience

The ATARI *Experience*

By
Adrien Z. Lamothe, Jr.

Edited by
William B. Sanders, Ph.D.

Illustrations by
Tes Bonnarith

DATAMOST™ INC
8943 Fullbright Ave., Chatsworth, CA 91311-2750
(818) 709-1202

DATAMOST INC™

ISBN 0-88190-239-X

TABLE OF CONTENTS

EDITOR'S INTRODUCTION

WILLIAM B. SANDERS, Ph.D.

How many times have you heard someone say, "but what can you do with your computer?" Such a question is an important one to consider when planning to purchase a home computer. For those who already own an Atari Home Computer, the question can be redirected to ask, "where do I begin in the long list of computer applications?"

In answer to these questions, there are three ways to learn how to operate your computer. They are; purchasing already written software programs, learning how to write your own individual software programs and learning how to program by keying in already written software programs.

This book represents the third alternative. It will help you learn about your computer and how to program it by copying programs. If you are not interested in learning how to program, you can simply key in the useful programs as they appear and save them to disk or tape. Either way, you will have several useful programs that you can use daily to help you with everything from simple daily chores to more complex business applications and utilities.

The best way to learn about your computer is to just sit down and become acquainted with it, and this book is designed to do just that!

Since Atari makes several excellent computers, you may wonder whether or not these programs will work on your particular Atari Home Computer. All of the programs contained in this book were written in Atari BASIC computing language. This means that any of the programs contained in this book will run with the version of BASIC that comes with the Atari computer. So if you own an Atari 400, 600XL, 800, 800XL, 1200XL, 1400XL, or 1450 XLD you can run any of the programs contained in this book. (On some of the Atari 400/800 models, BASIC is not included. You will need to get one to run any of these programs or any other BASIC program.)

The programs are written to be saved to disk, but can also be saved to tape. Some programs will need some minor line changes in order to save the program to tape, these are included where they may be needed. Therefore, no matter what type of Atari system configuration you may have, these programs will work on your Atari Home Computer.

The ATARI EXPERIENCE was designed to provide a wide range of applications to be of use to everyone. It is arranged into five distinct sections.

I	HOME
II	EDUCATION
III	ENTERTAINMENT
IV	BUSINESS
V	UTILITY PROGRAMS

The first section is a collection of programs that have a wide variety of applications in the home. Keeping track of birthdays, anniversaries, and special occasions can be done easily with DATE LOG. For your physical fitness, JOG LOG will help record your mileage and heart rate so you can see what shape you're in. Other programs in this section include Checkbook Balancer, Address Log, and Christmas Cards.

The Educational section contains an array of programs which will help develop children's skills in just about everything from math to capitals of each state of the union.

The third section, Entertainment, contains a number of games, as well as a drawing program to help create computer designs and graphics.

For the business minded person, this book contains several

decision making and financial planning programs. With these programs you can do everything from calculating profit to inventory tracking.

Finally, the last section of this book is devoted to utilities. “Utility” refers to a special type of program which can be used as an aid for another program. For example, in some operations, such as player/missile graphics, a special program is needed to transform binary numbers to decimal. In this section you will not only find this program, but also several other equally useful utilities.

As you can see, the ATARI EXPERIENCE is a true experience with a wide range of computer applications. What’s more, the programs can be modified to meet particular needs and tastes. All of the programs are clearly presented and explained, so if you want to change them, there is no mystery.

The author of the ATARI EXPERIENCE, Adrien Lamothe, has experience not only on the ATARI, but on other computers as well. With an eye for both clarity and practicality, Adrien has drafted this collection of programs so they could be used and understood by both novice and experienced programmers. He is currently pursuing a degree in computer science.

Section 1

Programs for the Home

- Checkbook Balancer
- Christmas Cards
- Address Log
- Date Log
- Jogging Log

PROGRAMS FOR THE HOME

The first section of this book is devoted to programs which can be used inside the home. The first program is a checkbook balancer; this can help balance and keep records from your checking account. The next program, Christmas card, will help you create Christmas cards for the holiday season. The final three programs in this section are logs designed to help organize information. The first of these is an address listing that allows the storage of names and addresses on disk. Next is a file which can be used to store important dates. The last program, the jogging log, can help formulate and plan a training regimen.

Checkbook Balancer

Do you have trouble balancing your checkbook? With this program you can use your Atari to keep your checking account in order. This program will do the math and keep track of your current balance under the file named CHKDATA.001. The program also assigns a password, specified by yourself, to restrict access to your data. As a further precaution, you can change the name of the data file to confuse anyone else looking for your account data.

If you plan to use the program for more than one account, simply rename the file reference statements for each account. Do this by changing the file name in lines 350, 530, and 1030. To avoid the effort involved in changing these lines every time you want to access a different account, save different versions of these lines as separate programs using the LIST command while leaving them out of the main program. When you ENTER the main program (save it using the LIST command) just enter the version of the file reference statements you need for your account.

```
10 REM *** CHECKBOOK BALANCER ***
20 REM
30 DIM A$(3), P$(8), R$(8)
40 C = 0
50 PRINT CHR$(125)
60 PRINT : PRINT "INSERT FILE DISK INTO DISK DRIVE."
70 PRINT "PRESS RETURN KEY WHEN READY."
80 INPUT A$
90 REM
100 REM ** Determine if old account. **
110 REM
120 PRINT CHR$(125)
130 PRINT : PRINT "Is this a new or old account?"
140 PRINT "(answer NEW or OLD)";
150 INPUT A$
160 IF A$ = "OLD" THEN 530
170 IF A$ <> "NEW" THEN 130
200 REM ****************
210 REM NEW ACCOUNT
220 REM ****************
230 PRINT CHR$(125)
240 PRINT
250 PRINT "Choose a password for your account"
260 PRINT "(use up to 8 letters or numbers)"
270 INPUT P$
280 PRINT CHR$(125)
290 PRINT : PRINT "What is your initial balance"
300 PRINT "(leave out the dollar sign)";
310 TRAP 290
320 INPUT B
330 B = INT(B * 100) / 100
340 REM Create datafile.
350 OPEN #1, 8, 0, "D:CHKDATA.001"
360 PRINT #1; B
370 PRINT #1; P$
380 CLOSE #1
390 PRINT CHR$(125)
```

```
400 PRINT : PRINT "Would you like to make a
transaction?"
410 PRINT "Answer Y or N";
420 INPUT A$
430 IF A$ = "Y" THEN 530
440 IF A$ <> "N" THEN 400
450 END
500 REM  ************************
510 REM TRANSACTION ROUTINE
520 REM  ************************
530 TRAP 50
540 OPEN #1, 4, 0, "D:CHKDATA.001"
550 INPUT #1; B
560 INPUT #1; P$
570 CLOSE #1
580 PRINT CHR$(125)
590 PRINT : PRINT "What is your password";
600 INPUT R$
610 C = C + 1
620 IF R$ = P$ THEN 660
630 IF C = 3 THEN END
640 PRINT : PRINT "That is not the password, try
again."
650 GOTO 590
660 PRINT CHR$(125)
670 PRINT : PRINT "SELECT TRANSACTION"
680 PRINT
690 PRINT "1) DEPOSIT"
700 PRINT "2) WITHDRAWAL"
710 PRINT "3) BALANCE INQUIRY"
720 TRAP 680
730 INPUT S
740 IF S < 1 OR S > 3 THEN 660
800 REM ********************
810 REM ADJUST BALANCE
820 REM ********************
830 ON S GOTO 840, 890, 930
840 PRINT CHR$(125)
```

```
850 PRINT : PRINT "Amount deposited (omit $)";
860 INPUT D
870 B = B + INT(D * 100) / 100
880 GOTO 950
890 PRINT CHR$(125)
900 PRINT : PRINT "Amount withdrawn (omit $)";
910 INPUT W
920 B = B - INT(W * 100) / 100
930 PRINT CHR$(125)
940 IF B < 0 THEN PRINT : PRINT "ACCOUNT
OVERDRAWN!"
950 PRINT : PRINT "Your balance is $";B
960 PRINT : PRINT "Another transaction (answer Y
or N)";
970 INPUT A$
980 IF A$ = "Y" THEN 660
990 IF A$ <> "N" THEN 960
1000 REM **************
1010 REM UPDATE FILE
1020 REM **************
1030 OPEN #1, 12, 0, "D: CHKDATA.001"
1040 PRINT #1; B
1050 CLOSE #1
1060 PRINT CHR$(125)
1070 PRINT : PRINT "Balance has been updated."
1080 PRINT "Program ended."
1090 END
```

Christmas Cards

Are you tired of shopping for Christmas cards every year? Why not let a printer, with some help from a computer, make cards for you? This program will print out personalized cards. You can print as many cards as you need. To print the cards you have to answer three questions: 1) the sender's name, 2) the current year, and 3) the quantity to be printed. When answering question 1, you can list more than one name. For example, you could answer "Jane and John Doe" or "The Does." Also, when you are finished printing you will have to fold each card.

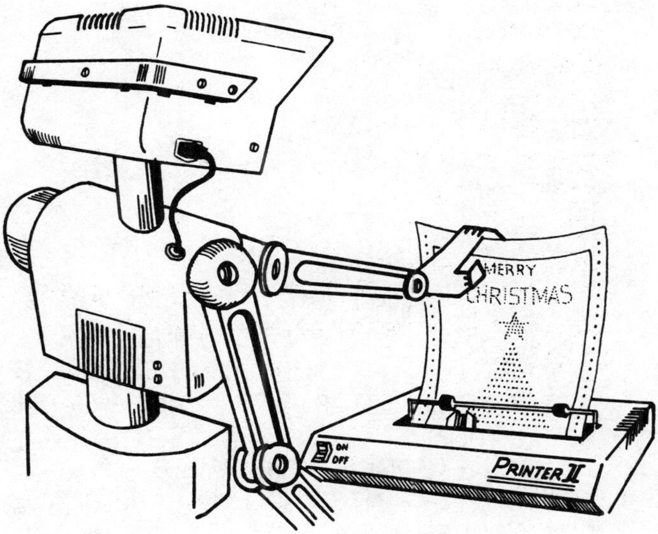

Lines 710, 1030 and 1130 control the formatting. If you experience problems with the cards' format, you can adjust these lines.

```
10 REM *** CHRISTMAS CARD ***
20 REM
30 DIM A$ (1), NAME$(32)
100 REM *************
110 REM USER DATA
120 REM *************
130 PRINT CHR$(125)
140 PRINT : PRINT "What is the name(s) of the
sender"
150 PRINT "(you may use up to 32 characters)"
160 INPUT NAME$
170 PRINT: PRINT "What is the current year";
180 TRAP 170
190 INPUT Y
200 IF Y < 1983 THEN 170
210 PRINT : PRINT "HOW MANY CARDS DO YOU
WISH TO PRINT";
220 TRAP 210
230 INPUT N
240 IF N <= 0 THEN 210
300 REM ****************
310 REM INSTRUCTIONS
320 REM ****************
330 FOR X = 1 TO N
340 PRINT CHR$ (125)
350 IF FLAG = 1 THEN GOTO 530
360 PRINT : PRINT "TURN ON THE PRINTER."
370 PRINT : PRINT "POSITION THE PRINT HEAD
AT THE TOP"
380 PRINT "EDGE OF THE PAPER."
390 PRINT : PRINT "WHEN YOU ARE READY TO
PRINT PRESS THE"
400 PRINT "RETURN KEY."
410 INPUT A$
420 IF N > 1 THEN FLAG = 1
500 REM *************
510 REM PRINT CARD
520 REM *************
```

```
530 LPRINT : LPRINT : LPRINT : LPRINT
540 LPRINT ,,,,," MERRY CHRISTMAS!"
550 LPRINT : LPRINT : LPRINT
560 LPRINT ,,,,,"          * "
570 LPRINT ,,,,,"         *** "
580 LPRINT ,,,,,"        ***** "
590 LPRINT ,,,,,"       ******* "
600 LPRINT ,,,,,"      ********* "
610 LPRINT ,,,,,"     *********** "
620 LPRINT ,,,,,"    ************* "
630 LPRINT ,,,,,"   *************** "
640 LPRINT ,,,,," *****************."
650 LPRINT ,,,,,"         *** "
660 LPRINT ,,,,,"         *** "
670 LPRINT ,,,,,"         *** "
680 LPRINT ,,,,,"         *** "
690 LPRINT : LPRINT : LPRINT
700 LPRINT ,,,,, "         AND A HAPPY NEW
YEAR!"
710 FOR J = 1 TO 41
720 LPRINT
730 NEXT J
740 NEXT X
800 REM *****************
810 REM INSTRUCTIONS
820 REM *****************
830 FOR X = 1 TO N
840 PRINT CHR$ (125)
850 IF FLAG2 = 1 THEN 1030
860 PRINT : PRINT "WAIT UNTIL THE PRINTER
HAS STOPPED."
870 PRINT : PRINT "REMOVE THE PAPER FROM
THE PRINTER."
880 PRINT : PRINT "REINSERT THE PAPER, ONLY
FEED THE"
890 PRINT "BOTTOM EDGE IN FIRST."
900 PRINT "POSITION THE PRINT HEAD AT THE
TOP OF"
```

```
910 PRINT "THE PAPER."
920 PRINT : PRINT "WHEN YOU ARE READY TO
PRINT PRESS THE"
930 PRINT "RETURN KEY."
940 INPUT A$
950 IF N > 1 THEN FLAG 2 = 1
1000 REM ******************
1010 REM PRINT MESSAGE
1020 REM ******************
1030 FOR J = 1 TO 10
1040 LPRINT
1050 NEXT J
1060 LPRINT ,,,,"                A very Merry
Christmas to you and"
1070 LPRINT ,,,,"          yours."
1080 LPRINT ,,,,"          May you enjoy the best of
health"
1090 LPRINT ,,,,"          and may ";Y+1;" be your
best year"
1100 LPRINT ,,,,"          yet."
1110 LPRINT
1120 LPRINT ,,,,"          Yours truly,"
1130 LPRINT
1140 ,,,,"          ";NAME$
1150 FOR J = 1 TO 47
1160 LPRINT
1170 NEXT J
1180 NEXT X
1200 REM ************
1210 REM RUN AGAIN?
1220 REM ************
1230 PRINT : PRINT "DO YOU WISH TO RUN THE
PROGRAM AGAIN?"
1240 PRINT "ANSWER Y OR N";
1250 INPUT A$
1260 IF A$ = "Y" THEN 130
1270 IF A$ <> "N" THEN 1240
1280 PRINT : PRINT "PROGRAM ENDED."
1290 END
```

Address Log

This program is a computerized address book. The program stores addresses in a file named ADDRESS.DAT. Using the program you can add, delete, or update the information in the log. Each record has six fields: 1) name, 2) address, 3) city, 4) state, 5) zip code, and 6) telephone number. There are limits on the number of characters you can use for each field. The name field cannot exceed 24 characters. The address and city fields cannot exceed 38 and 16 characters, respectively. When entering the state, use the two letter code. The telephone number field cannot exceed 14 characters. The reason for these limits is because a string greater than 99 characters in length cannot be sorted.

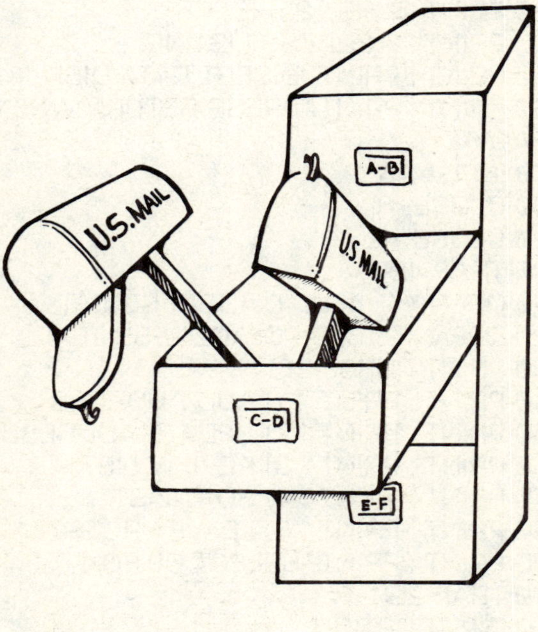

When you access the file you have two options: 1) display the entire file, or 2) display a particular record. When you want to display one record you must enter the person's name exactly the way it is stored in the file. Otherwise, the program will not recognize the record you want and it won't be displayed. Also, if you want your file to be sorted by last names, you will have to enter them last name first.

```
10 REM *** ADDRESS LISTING ***
20 REM
30 DIM A$(24), B$(1), NAME$(24), ADDR$(38),
CITY$(16), STATE$(2)
40 DIM ZIP$(5), TEL$(14), ELEM$(99),
FILE$(10000), REC$(38)
50 DIM ADDLEN(1000), CITLEN(1000)
100 REM *************
110 REM USER INPUT
120 REM *************
130 PRINT CHR$(125)
140 PRINT ,"ADDRESS LISTING"
150 PRINT : PRINT "INSERT DATA DISK."
160 PRINT : PRINT "PRESS RETURN WHEN
READY";
170 INPUT A$
180 CLOSE #1
190 CLOSE #2
200 TRAP 400
210 OPEN #1, 4, 0, "D:ADDRESS.DAT"
220 OPEN #2, 8, 0, "D: ADDRESS TEM"
230 PRINT CHR$(125)
240 PRINT : PRINT " 1) ADD ADDRESS"
250 PRINT : PRINT " 2) UPDATE ADDRESS"
260 PRINT : PRINT " 3) REVIEW LIST"
270 PRINT : PRINT " 4) SORT LIST"
280 PRINT : PRINT " 5) LEAVE PROGRAM"
290 PRINT : PRINT "SELECT OPTION";
300 TRAP 290
310 INPUT OPTION
```

```
320 IF OPTION < 1 OR OPTION > 5 THEN 290
330 ON OPTION GOTO 700, 1300, 1600, 2010, 340
340 CLOSE #1
350 CLOSE #2
360 PRINT : PRINT "FILES CLOSED, PROGRAM
ENDED."
370 END
400 REM ******************
410 REM FILE NOT FOUND
420 REM ******************
430 PRINT CHR$(253);
440 PRINT : PRINT "FILE NOT FOUND ON THIS
DISK."
450 PRINT : PRINT "Either insert proper disk and
enter"
460 PRINT "'NEW' or enter 'CREATE' to create a"
470 PRINT "new file on this disk";
480 INPUT A$
490 IF A$ = "NEW" THEN 190
500 IF A$ <> "CREATE" THEN 450
600 REM *******************
610 REM CREATE NEW FILE
620 REM *******************
630 CLOSE #1
640 OPEN #1, 8, 0, "D:ADDRESS.DAT"
650 PRINT #1; "END"
660 CLOSE #1
670 GOTO 180
700 REM ***********************
710 REM TRANSFER RECORDS
720 REM ***********************
730 COUNT = 0
740 INPUT #1; NAME$
750 IF NAME$ = "END" THEN 900
760 PRINT #2; NAME$
770 INPUT #1; ADDR$
780 PRINT #2; ADDR$
790 INPUT #1; CITY$
```

```
800 PRINT #2; CITY$
810 INPUT #1; STATE$
820 PRINT #2; STATE$
830 INPUT #1; ZIP$
840 PRINT #2; ZIP$
850 INPUT #1; TEL$
860 PRINT #2; TEL$
870 COUNT = COUNT + 1
880 GOTO 740
900 REM *********************
910 REM ADD APPOINTMENT
920 REM *********************
930 PRINT CHR$(125)
940 IF OPTION = 1 THEN PRINT "ADD ADDRESS"
950 IF OPTION = 2 THEN PRINT "CHANGE
ADDRESS" : GOTO 970
960 PRINT : PRINT "ENTER 'END' WHEN DONE."
970 PRINT : PRINT "NAME....";
980 INPUT NAME$
990 IF NAME$ = "END" THEN 2700
1000 IF LEN(NAME$) < 1 THEN 970
1010 PRINT : PRINT "ADDRESS....";
1020 INPUT ADDR$
1030 IF LEN(ADDR$) < 1 THEN 1010
1040 PRINT : PRINT "CITY.......";
1050 INPUT CITY$
1060 IF LEN(CITY$) < 1 THEN 1040
1070 PRINT : PRINT "STATE......";
1080 INPUT STATE$
1090 IF LEN(STATE$) < 1 THEN 1110
1100 PRINT : PRINT "ZIP........";
1110 INPUT ZIP$
1120 IF LEN(ZIP$) < 1 THEN 1100
1130 PRINT : PRINT "PHONE......";
1140 INPUT TEL$
1150 IF LEN(TEL$) < 1 THEN 1130
1160 PRINT : PRINT " 1) ADD"
1170 PRINT : PRINT " 2) CHANGE"
```

```
1180 PRINT : PRINT "SELECT OPTION";
1190 TRAP 1180
1200 INPUT OPT2
1210 IF OPT2 < 1 OR OPT2 > 2 THEN 1180
1220 IF OPT2 = 2 THEN 900
1230 IF OPTION = 1 THEN COUNT = COUNT + 1
1240 GOTO 2600
1300 REM  *****************
1310 REM READ RECORDS
1320 REM  *****************
1330 COUNT = 0
1340 INPUT #1; NAME$
1350 IF NAME$ = "END" THEN 2700
1360 INPUT #1; ADDR$
1370 INPUT #1; CITY$
1380 INPUT #1; STATE$
1390 INPUT #1; ZIP$
1400 INPUT #1; TEL$
1410 COUNT = COUNT + 1
1420 PRINT CHR$(125)
1430 PRINT : PRINT "NAME.......": NAME$
1440 PRINT : PRINT "ADDRESS....": ADDR$
1450 PRINT : PRINT "CITY.......": CITY$
1460 PRINT : PRINT "STATE......": STATE$
1470 PRINT : PRINT "ZIP........": ZIP$
1480 PRINT : PRINT "PHONE......": TEL$
1490 PRINT : PRINT " 1) KEEP"
1500 PRINT : PRINT " 2) CHANGE"
1510 PRINT : PRINT " 3) DELETE"
1520 PRINT : PRINT "SELECT OPTION";
1530 TRAP 1520
1540 INPUT OPT2
1550 IF OPT2 < 1 OR OPT2 > 3 THEN 1520
1560 IF OPT 2 = 3 THEN COUNT = COUNT - 1
1570 ON OPT2 GOTO 2600, 900, 1340
1600 REM **************
1610 REM REVIEW LOG
1620 REM **************
```

```
1630 PRINT CHR$(125)
1640 PRINT "Enter the name you want to review"
1650 PRINT "or enter 'ALL' to review the entire"
1660 PRINT "listing";
1670 INPUT A$
1680 NUM = 0
1690 PRINT CHR$(125)
1700 IF A$ = "ALL" THEN 1710
1710 INPUT #1; NAME$
1720 IF NAME$ = "END" THEN 1890
1730 INPUT #1; ADDR$
1740 INPUT #1; CITY$
1750 INPUT #1; STATE$
1760 INPUT #1; ZIP$
1770 INPUT #1; TEL$
1780 IF A$ = "ALL" THEN 1800
1790 IF A$ <> NAME$ THEN 1710
1800 PRINT NAME$
1810 PRINT ADDR$
1820 PRINT CITY$; ", "; STATE$; " ";ZIP
1830 PRINT "TEL.: "; TEL$
1840 PRINT
1850 NUM = NUM + 1
1860 IF NUM = 3 THEN PRINT : PRINT
"PRESS RETURN TO CONTINUE"; : INPUT B$
1870 IF NUM = 3 THEN NUM = 0 : PRINT
CHR$(125)
1880 GOTO 1710
1890 PRINT : PRINT "PRESS RETURN WHEN
FINISHED";
1900 INPUT A$
1910 GOTO 2760
2000 REM ***********
2010 REM SORT LOG
2020 REM ***********
2030 INPUT #1; REC$
2040 IF REC$ = "END" THEN 2060
2050 GOTO 2030
```

```
2060 INPUT #1; COUNT
2070 CLOSE #1
2080 IF COUNT < 2 THEN PRINT : PRINT "SORT
NOT REQUIRED." : GOTO 180
2090 PRINT : PRINT "STANDBY WHILE FILE IS
SORTED."
2100 FOR J = 1 TO COUNT * 99 : FILE$(J, J) = "
" : NEXT J
2110 I = 1
2120 COUNT = 1
2130 OPEN #1, 4, 0, "D:ADDRESS.DAT"
2140 INPUT #1; NAME$
2150 IF NAME$ = "END" THEN 2320
2160 FILE$ (I, I + 23) = NAME$
2170 INPUT #1; ADDR$
2180 ADDLEN(COUNT) = LEN(ADDR$)
2190 FILE$(I + 24, I + 61) = ADDR$
2200 INPUT #1; CITY$
2210 FILE$(I + 62, I + 77) = CITY$
2220 CITLEN(COUNT) = LEN(CITY$)
2230 INPUT #1; STATE$
2240 FILE$(I + 78, I + 79) = STATE$
2250 INPUT #1; ZIP$
2260 FILE$(I + 80, I + 84) = ZIP$
2270 INPUT #1; TEL$
2280 FILE $(I + 85, I + 98) = TEL$
2290 I = I + 99
2300 COUNT = COUNT + 1
2310 GOTO 2140
2320 STRING = (COUNT - 2) * 99
2330 FOR N = 1 TO COUNT - 1
2340 FOR P = 1 TO STRING - 98 STEP 99
2350 PL = P + 98
2360 PLEN = P + 99
2370 PLEN1 = P + 197
2380 IF FILE$(P, PL) <= FILE$(PLEN, PLEN1)
THEN 2420
2390 ELEM$ = FILE$(P, PL)
```

```
2400 FILE$(P, PL) = FILE$(PLEN, PLEN1)
2410 FILE$(PLEN, PLEN1) = ELEM$
2420 NEXT P
2430 NEXT N
2440 I = 1
2450 X = 1
2460 IF X > COUNT - 1 THEN 2700
2470 NAME$ = FILE$(I, I + 23)
2480 ADDR$ = FILE$(I + 24, I + 61)
2490 ADDR$ = ADDR$(1, ADDLEN(X))
2500 CITY$ = FILE$(I + 62, I + 77)
2510 STAT      = FILE$(I + 78, I + 79)
2520 ZIP$ = FILE$(I + 80, I + 84)
2530 CITY$ = CITY$(1, CITLEN(X))
2540 TEL$ = FILE$(I + 85, I + 98)
2550 I = I + 99
2560 X = X + 1
2600 REM **********************
2610 REM WRITE TO NEW FILE
2620 REM **********************
2630 PRINT #2; NAME$
2640 PRINT #2; ADDR$
2650 PRINT #2; CITY$
2660 PRINT #2; STATE$
2670 PRINT #2; ZIP$
2680 PRINT #2; TEL$
2690 ON OPTION GOTO 930, 1340, 1600, 2460, 340
2700 REM  ******************
2710 REM CLOSE FILES
2720 REM  ******************
2730 PRINT : PRINT "STANDBY WHILE FILES ARE
CLOSED."
2740 PRINT #2; "END"
2750 PRINT #2; COUNT
2760 CLOSE #1
2770 CLOSE #2
2780 IF OPTION = 3 THEN 2810
2790 XIO 33, #1, 0, 0, "D:ADDRESS.DAT"
```

```
2800 XIO 32, #1, 0, 0, "D:ADDRESS.TEM,
ADDRESS.DAT"
2810 GOTO 210
```

Date Log

Have you ever forgotten a wedding anniversary or birthday? With this program you can establish a log of all the important dates you want to remember. The program stores the information on a disk file named DATE.DAT. This program allows several options. You can add, change, and delete items in the log. Items can be sorted so they will appear in chronological order. Each record in the file consists of two fields: a date field and an occasion field. When entering a date, use the format MMDD where MM is the month (01 to 12) and DD is the day (01 to 31). It's important to enter the date in this format so records will sort properly. The occasion field cannot exceed 34 characters, this allows for clear viewing on a 40 column screen. If you have an 80 column card you can expand the occasion field by making the following line changes:

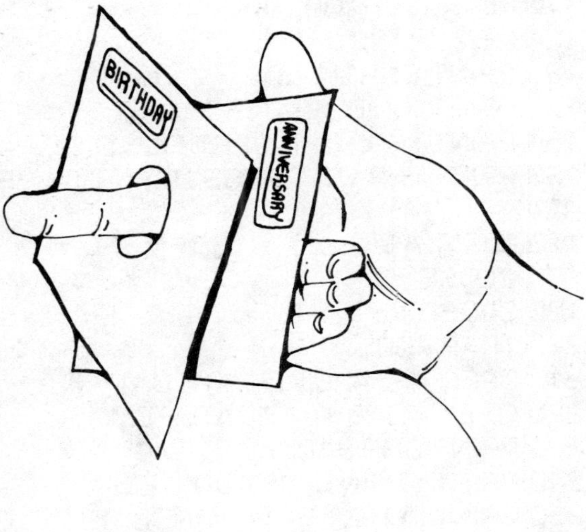

```
30 DIM A$(6), DATE$(4), OCC$(74)
40 DIM REC$(74), FILE$(10000),ELEM$(78)
1060 IF LEN (OCC$) > 74 THEN 810
1800 FOR J = 1 TO COUNT * 78
1890 FILE$(I + 4, I + 77) = OCC$
1900 I = I + 78
1920 STRING = (COUNT - 1) * 78
1940 FOR P = 1 TO STRING - 77 STEP 78
1950 PL = P + 77
1960 PLEN = P + 78
1970 PLEN1 = P + 155
2080 OCC$ = FILE (I + 4, I + 77)
2090 I = I + 78
```

```
10 REM *** DATE LOG ***
20 REM
30 DIM A$(6), B$(1), DATE$(4), OCC$(65)
40 DIM REC$(65), FILE$(10000), ELEM$(69)
100 REM  *************
110 REM USER INPUT
120 REM  *************
130 PRINT CHR$(125)
140 PRINT ,"IMPORTANT DATES"
150 PRINT : PRINT "INSERT FILE DISK."
160 PRINT : PRINT "PRESS RETURN WHEN
READY";
170 INPUT A$
180 CLOSE #1
190 CLOSE #2
200 TRAP 400
210 OPEN #1, 4, 0, "D:DATE.DAT"
220 OPEN #2, 8, 0, "D:DATE.TEM"
230 PRINT CHR$(125)
240 PRINT : PRINT " 1) ADD ITEM"
250 PRINT : PRINT " 2) CHANGE OR DELETE
ITEM"
260 PRINT : PRINT " 3) REVIEW ITEM(S)"
270 PRINT : PRINT " 4) SORT LOG"
```

```
280 PRINT : PRINT " 5) LEAVE PROGRAM"
290 PRINT : PRINT "SELECT OPTION";
300 TRAP 290
310 INPUT OPTION
320 IF OPTION < 1 OR OPTION > 5 THEN 290
330 ON OPTION GOTO 700, 1200, 1400, 1700, 340
340 CLOSE #1
350 CLOSE #2
360 PRINT : PRINT "FILES CLOSED, PROGRAM
ENDED."
370 END
400 REM ******************
410 REM FILE NOT FOUND
420 REM ******************
430 PRINT CHR$(253);
440 PRINT : PRINT "FILE NOT FOUND ON THIS
DISK."
450 PRINT : PRINT "Either insert proper disk and
enter"
460 PRINT "'NEW' or enter 'CREATE' to create a"
470 PRINT "new file on this disk";
480 INPUT A$
490 IF A$ = "NEW" THEN 180
500 IF A$ <> "CREATE" THEN 450
600 REM  *******************
610 REM CREATE NEW FILE
620 REM  *******************
630 CLOSE #1
640 OPEN #1, 8, 0, "D:DATE.DAT"
650 PRINT #1; "END"
660 CLOSE #1
670 POKE 195, 0
680 GOTO 180
700 REM ************************
710 REM TRANSFER RECORDS
720 REM ************************
730 COUNT = 0
740 INPUT #1; DATE$
```

```
750 IF DATE$ = "END" THEN 900
760 PRINT #2; DATE$
770 INPUT #1; OCC$
780 PRINT #2; OCC$
790 COUNT = COUNT + 1
800 GOTO 740
900 REM ***********
910 REM ADD ITEM
920 REM ***********
930 PRINT CHR$(125)
940 IF OPTION = 1 THEN PRINT "ADD ITEM"
950 IF OPTION = 2 THEN PRINT "CHANGE ITEM"
: GOTO 970
960 PRINT : PRINT "ENTER 'END' WHEN DONE."
970 PRINT : PRINT "DATE ...........";
980 INPUT DATE$
990 IF OPTION = 2 THEN 1010
1000 IF DATE$ = "END" THEN 2300
1010 IF LEN(DATE$) <> 4 THEN 970
1020 IF VAL(DATE$) < 101 THEN 970
1030 IF VAL(DATE$) > 1231 THEN 970
1040 PRINT: PRINT "OCCASION......";
1050 INPUT OCC$
1060 IF LEN(OCC$) > 65 THEN 1040
1070 PRINT : PRINT " 1) ADD"
1080 PRINT : PRINT " 2) CHANGE"
1090 PRINT : PRINT "SELECT OPTION";
1100 TRAP 1090
1110 INPUT OPT2
1120 IF OPT2 < 1 OR OPT2 > 2 THEN 1100
1130 IF OPT2 = 2 THEN 900
1140 IF OPTION = 1 THEN COUNT = COUNT + 1
1150 GOTO 2200
1200 REM *****************
1210 REM READ RECORDS
1220 REM *****************
1230 COUNT = 0
1240 INPUT #1; DATE$
```

```
1250 IF DATE$ = “END” THEN 2300
1260 INPUT #1; OCC$
1270 COUNT = COUNT + 1
1280 PRINT CHR$(125)
1290 PRINT : PRINT “ITEM #. . . . ”; DATE$
1300 PRINT : PRINT “ITEM. . . . . .”; OCC$
1310 PRINT : PRINT “ 1) KEEP”
1320 PRINT : PRINT “ 2) CHANGE”
1330 PRINT : PRINT “ 3) DELETE”
1340 PRINT : PRINT “SELECT OPTION”;
1350 TRAP 1340
1360 INPUT OPT2
1370 IF OPT 2 < 1 OR OPT2 > 3 THEN 1340
1380 IF OPT2 = 3 THEN COUNT = COUNT - 1
1390 ON OPT2 GOTO 2200, 900, 1240
1400 REM ****************
1430 REM REVIEW ITEMS
1440 REM ****************
1430 PRINT CHR$(125)
1440 PRINT : PRINT “Enter the date you want to review”
1450 PRINT “or enter ALL to review the entire log”;
1460 TRAP 1440
1470 INPUT A$
1480 IF A$ = “ALL” THEN 1520
1490 IF LEN(A$) <> 4 THEN 1440
1500 IF VAL(A$) < 101 THEN 1440
1510 IF VAL(A$) > 1231 THEN 1440
1520 PRINT CHR$(125)
1530 INPUT #1; DATE$
1540 IF DATE$ = “END” THEN 1650
1550 INPUT #1; OCC$
1560 IF A$ = “ALL” THEN 1580
1570 IF A$ <> DATE$ THEN 1530
1580 PRINT “DATE ............”; DATE$
1590 PRINT “OCCASION...... ”; OCC$
1600 PRINT
1610 ITEM = ITEM + 1
```

```
1620 IF ITEM = 4 THEN PRINT :
PRINT "PRESS RETURN TO
CONTINUE"; : INPUT B$
1630 IF ITEM = 4 THEN ITEM = 0 :
GOTO 1520
1640 GOTO 1530
1650 PRINT : PRINT "PRESS
RETURN WHEN FINISHED"; : INPUT
A$
1660 GOTO 2330
1700 REM ************
1710 REM SORT LIST
1720 REM ************
1730 INPUT #1; REC$
1740 IF REC$ = "END" THEN 1760
1750 GOTO 1730
1760 INPUT #1; COUNT
1770 CLOSE #1
1780 IF COUNT < 2 THEN PRINT : PRINT "SORT
NOT REQUIRED." : GOTO 180
1790 PRINT : PRINT "STANDBY WHILE FILE IS
SORTED."
1800 FOR J = 1 TO COUNT * 69
1810 FILE$(J, J) = " "
1820 NEXT J
1830 I = 1
1840 OPEN #1, 4, 0, "D:DATE.DAT"
1850 INPUT #1; DATE$
1860 IF DATE$ = "END" THEN 1920
1870 FILE$(I, I + 3) = DATE$
1880 INPUT #1; OCC$
1890 FILE$(I + 4, I + 68) = OCC$
1900 I = I + 69
1910 GOTO 1850
1920 STRING = (COUNT - 1) * 69
1930 FOR N = 1 TO COUNT - 1
1940 FOR P = 1 TO STRING - 68 STEP 69
1950 PL = P + 68
```

```
1960 PLEN = P + 69
1970 PLEN1 = P + 137
1980 IF FILE$(P, PL) <= FILE$(PLEN, PLEN1)
THEN 2020
1990 ELEM$ = FILE$(P, PL)
2000 FILE$(P, PL) = FILE$(PLEN, PLEN1)
2010 FILE$(PLEN, PLEN1) = ELEM$
2020 NEXT P
2030 NEXT N
2040 I = 1
2050 X = 1
2060 IF X > COUNT THEN 2300
2070 DATE$ = FILE$(I, I + 3)
2080 OCC$ = FILE$(I + 4, I + 68)
2090 I = I + 69
2100 X = X + 1
2200 REM **********************
2210 REM WRITE TO NEW FILE
2220 REM **********************
2230 PRINT #2; DATE$
2240 PRINT #2; OCC$
2250 ON OPTION GOTO 930, 1240, 180, 2060, 340
2300 REM  **************
2310 REM CLOSE FILES
2320 REM  **************
2330 PRINT : PRINT "STANDBY WHILE FILES ARE
CLOSED."
2340 PRINT #2; "END"
2350 PRINT #2; COUNT
2360 CLOSE #1
2370 CLOSE #2
2380 IF OPTION = 3 THEN 180
2390 XIO 33, #1, 0, 0, "D:DATE.DAT"
2400 XIO 32, #1, 0, 0, "D:DATE.TEM, DATE.DAT"
2410 GOTO 180
```

Jogging Log

This program can keep track of all the miles you run, it also records your resting pulse rate and weight. This is useful information because you can chart how running is affecting your health.

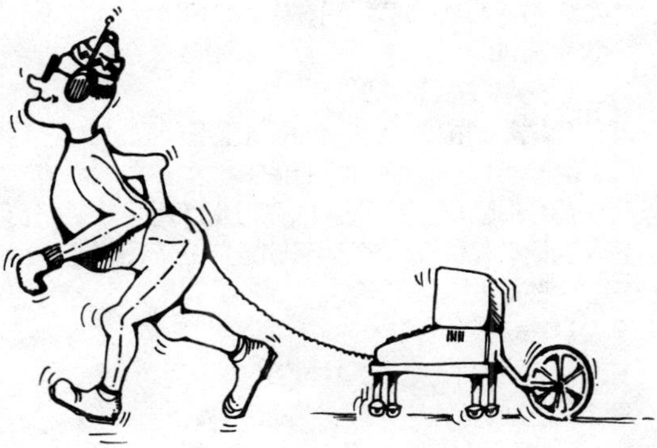

Each entry made in the log represents one week of activity. The log divides a calendar year into 52 weeks or 52 entries. To figure out what the current week is, take the Julian date (1 – 365) and divide by 7. Use the Julian date program in the Utility Section of this book to find the current Julian date.

This program also has an option which allows you to display the log using a line graph. The top line represents your mileage. The center line shows your pulse rate and the bottom line your weight. With the graph you can visualize the weekly fluctuations in your mileage, pulse, and weight. The information in the log is helpful in avoiding overtraining. If you are increasing your mileage sharply and your weight is decreasing sharply and your resting pulse rate is increasing you are over training. If you back off on the mileage your pulse should drop and weight increase.

Keeping a log also helps optimize your training. Many people feel they have to constantly increase their mileage. If you keep your mileage constant from week to week your pulse and weight will usually continue to gradually decrease. When your pulse and weight remain constant, then it is time to increase mileage. At that point, your body will be in good enough condition to handle the extra miles with a decreased chance of injury.

```
10 REM *** JOGGING LOG ***
20 REM
30 GRAPHICS 0
40 DIM MILES(52), PULSE(52), WEIGHT(52),
S(52), C(52), FLAG(52)
50 DIM MPLOT(52), PPLOT(52), WPLOT(52)
60 DIM A$(5), YEAR$(4), EXT$(3), FILE1$(13),
FILE2$(12)
70 REM
80 REM ** SET FLAG(N) TO 0 **
90 REM
100 FOR N = 2 TO 52
110 FLAG(N) = 0
120 NEXT N
200 REM **************
210 REM USER INPUT
220 REM **************
230 PRINT CHR$(125)
240 PRINT ,"JOGGING LOG"
250 PRINT : PRINT "Start a new file (Y or N)";
260 INPUT A$
270 IF A$ = "N" THEN 340
280 IF A$ <> "Y" THEN 250
290 PRINT : PRINT "What year will the file cover";
300 TRAP 290
310 INPUT YEAR
320 X = 1
330 GOTO 380
340 PRINT : PRINT "What year do you want to
access";
```

```
350 TRAP 340
360 INPUT YEAR
370 X = 2
380 YEAR$ = STR$(YEAR)
390 IF LEN(YEAR$) <> 4 THEN ON X GOTO 290, 340
400 EXT$ = YEAR$(2, 4)
410 FILE1$(1, 10) = "D:JOGDATA."
420 FILE2$(1, 9) = "D:JOGKEY."
430 FILE1$(11, 13) = EXT$
440 FILE2$(10, 12) = EXT$
450 ON X GOTO 530, 800
500 REM ******************
510 REM CREATE DATAFILE
520 REM ******************
530 OPEN #1, 8, 0, FILE1$
540 PRINT #1; YEAR
550 FOR WEEK = 1 TO 52
560 NOTE #1, S, C
570 S(WEEK) = S
580 C(WEEK) = C
590 MILES(WEEK) = 999
600 PRINT #1; MILES(WEEK)
610 PULSE(WEEK) = 999
620 PRINT #1; PULSE(WEEK)
630 WEIGHT(WEEK) = 999
640 PRINT #1; WEIGHT(WEEK)
650 NEXT WEEK
660 CLOSE #1
700 REM ******************
710 REM CREATE KEY FILE
720 REM ******************
730 OPEN #1, 8, 0, FILE2$
740 FOR WEEK = 1 TO 52
750 PRINT #1; S(WEEK)
760 PRINT #1; C(WEEK)
770 NEXT WEEK
780 CLOSE #1
790 GOTO 900
```

```
800 PRINT CHR$(125)
810 PRINT : PRINT "Do you want to make an entry
or just"
820 PRINT "review the current data (answer ENT"
830 PRINT "or REV)";
840 INPUT A$
850 IF A$ = "REV" THEN 1760
860 IF A$ <> "ENT" THEN 800
900 REM ******************
910 REM ENTRY ROUTINE
920 REM ******************
930 FLAG = 2
940 PRINT CHR$(125)
950 PRINT : PRINT "What week is it";
960 TRAP 950
970 INPUT WEEK
980 IF WEEK < 1 OR WEEK > 52 THEN 950
990 PRINT : PRINT "How many miles did you run
this"
1000 PRINT "week";
1010 TRAP 990
1020 INPUT MILES
1030 IF MILES < 1 OR MILES > 198 THEN 990
1040 PRINT : PRINT "What was your resting pulse
rate at"
1050 PRINT "the end of the week";
1060 TRAP 1040
1070 INPUT PULSE
1080 IF PULSE < 25 OR PULSE > 198 THEN 1040
1090 PRINT : PRINT "How much did you weight at
weeks"
1100 PRINT "end";
1110 TRAP 1090
1120 INPUT WEIGHT
1130 IF WEIGHT < 50 OR WEIGHT > 500 THEN
1090
1140 PRINT CHR$(125)
```

```
1150 PRINT : PRINT "WEEK", "MILES", "PULSE",
"WEIGHT"
1160 PRINT : PRINT WEEK, MILES, PULSE,
WEIGHT
1170 PRINT : PRINT "Is this information correct
(answer"
1180 PRINT "(Y or N)";
1190 INPUT A$
1200 IF A$ = "N" THEN 900
1210 IF A$ <> "Y" THEN 1170
1300 REM **************
1310 REM UPDATE FILE
1320 REM **************
1330 REM
1340 REM ** INPUT KEY FILE **
1350 REM
1360 OPEN #1, 4, 0, FILE2$
1370 FOR N = 1 TO 52
1380 INPUT #1; S
1390 S(N) = S
1400 INPUT #1; C
1410 C(N) = C
1420 NEXT N
1430 CLOSE #1
1440 REM
1450 REM ** UPDATE DATA FILE **
1460 REM
1470 OPEN #1, 12, 0, FILE1$
1480 S = S(WEEK)
1490 C = C(WEEK)
1500 POINT #1, S, C
1510 MILES(WEEK) = MILES+100
1520 PRINT #1; MILES(WEEK)
1530 PULSE(WEEK) = PULSE+100
1540 PRINT #1; PULSE(WEEK)
1550 WEIGHT(WEEK) = WEIGHT+100
1560 PRINT #1; WEIGHT(WEEK)
1570 CLOSE #1
```

```
1580 IF FLAG <> 2 THEN 1630
1590 PRINT : PRINT "Another entry (Y or N)";
1600 INPUT A$
1610 IF A$ = "Y" THEN 940
1620 IF A$ <> "N" THEN 1590
1630 PRINT CHR$(125)
1640 PRINT : PRINT "Do you want to review the
log";
1650 INPUT A$
1660 IF A$ = "N" THEN FLAG = 1 : GOTO 2110
1670 IF A$ <> "Y" THEN 1640
1700 REM **************
1710 REM REVIEW FILE
1720 REM **************
1730 REM
1740 REM ** INPUT FILE **
1750 REM
1760 OPEN #1, 4, 0, FILE1$
1770 INPUT #1; YEAR
1780 FOR WEEK = 1 TO 52
1790 INPUT #1; MILES
1800 IF MILES = 999 THEN MILES = 0 : GOTO 1820
1810 MILES = MILE -100
1820 MILES(WEEK) = MILES
1830 INPUT #1; PULSE
1840 IF PULSE = 999 THEN PULSE =  : GOTO
1860
1850 PULSE = PULSE - 100
1860 PULSE(WEEK) = PULSE
1870 INPUT #1; WEIGHT
1880 IF WEIGHT = 999 THEN WEIGHT = 0 :
GOTO 1900
1890 WEIGHT = WEIGHT - 100
1900 WEIGHT(WEEK) = WEIGHT
1910 NEXT WEEK
1920 CLOSE #1
1930 IF FLAG = 1 THEN 2230
1940 REM
```

```
1950 REM ** OUTPUT FILE **
1960 REM
1970 PRINT CHR$(125)
1980 PRINT : PRINT ,"JOGGING LOG FOR "; YEAR
1990 PRINT : PRINT "WEEK", "MILES", "PULSE",
"WEIGHT"
2000 FOR WEEK = 1 TO 52
2010 PRINT WEEK, MILES(WEEK), PULSE(WEEK),
WEIGHT(WEEK)
2020 ROW = PEEK(84)
2030 IF ROW >= 20 THEN PRINT : PRINT
"PRESS RETURN TO CONTINUE REVIEW";
2040 TRAP 2060
2050 IF ROW >= 20 THEN INPUT A$
2060 ERROR = PEEK(195)
2070 IF ERROR <> 8 AND ERROR <> 0 THEN
PRINT : PRINT "ERROR- "; ERROR : END
2080 IF ERROR = 8 THEN 2030
2090 IF ROW >= 20 THEN PRINT CHR$(125)
2100 NEXT WEEK
2110 PRINT : PRINT "Do you want to review the
data on a"
2120 PRINT "line graph (answer Y or N)";
2130 INPUT A$
2140 IF A$ = "Y" AND FLAG = 1 THEN 1700
2150 IF A$ = "Y" THEN 2230
2160 IF A$ <> "N" THEN 1760
2170 PRINT : PRINT "PROGRAM ENDED"
2180 END
2200 REM ********************
2210 REM DRAW LINE GRAPH
2220 REM ********************
2230 GRAPHICS 7
2240 REM
2250 REM ** FIND HIGH/LOW VALUES **
2260 REM
2270 FOR WEEK = 1 TO 52
2280 IF MILES(WEEK) > MHIGH THEN MHIGH =
```

```
MILES(WEEK)
2290 IF PULSE(WEEK) > PHIGH THEN PHIGH =
PULSE(WEEK)
2300 IF WEIGHT(WEEK) > WHIGH THEN WHIGH
= WEIGHT(WEEK)
2310 IF MILES(WEEK) <= MLOW THEN MLOW =
MILES(WEEK)
2320 IF PULSE(WEEK) <= PLOW THEN PLOW =
PULSE(WEEK)
2330 IF WEIGHT(WEEK) <= WLOW THEN WLOW
= WEIGHT(WEEK)
2340 NEXT WEEK
2350 REM
2360 REM ** FIND RANGE **
2370 REM
2380 MRANGE = MHIGH - MLOW
2390 PRANGE = PHIGH - PLOW
2400 WRANGE = WHIGH - WLOW
2410 REM
2420 REM ** FIND SCALE **
2430 REM
2440 MSCALE = MRANGE / 20
2450 PSCALE = PRANGE / 20
2460 WSCALE = WRANGE/20
2470 REM
2480 REM ** ASSIGN Y VALUE TO DATA **
2490 REM
2500 FOR WEEK = 1 TO 52
2510 MPLOT(WEEK) = 24 - (MILES(WEEK) -
MLOW) / MSCALE
2520 PPLOT(WEEK) = 49 - (PULSE(WEEK) -
PLOW) / PSCALE
2530 WPLOT(WEEK) = 74 - (WEIGHT(WEEK) -
WLOW) / WSCALE
2540 NEXT WEEK
2550 REM
2560 REM ** DRAW PULSE RATE LINE **
2570 REM
```

```
2580 COLOR 1
2590 PLOT 3, PPLOT(1)
2600 FOR WEEK = 2 TO 52
2610 IF PPLOT(WEEK) = 49 THEN FLAG(WEEK)
= 1 : PLOT 3 * WEEK, PPLOT(WEEK)
2620 IF PPLOT(WEEK) = 49 THEN 2640
2630 DRAWTO 3 * WEEK, PPLOT(WEEK)
2640 NEXT WEEK
2560 REM
2660 REM ** DRAW MILEAGE LINE **
2670 REM
2680 COLOR 1
2690 PLOT 3, MPLOT(1)
2700 FOR WEEK = 2 TO 52
2710 IF FLAG(WEEK) = 1 THEN PLOT 3 * WEEK,
MPLOT(WEEK) : GOTO 2730
2720 DRAWTO 3 * WEEK, MPLOT(WEEK)
2730 NEXT WEEK
2740 REM
2750 REM ** DRAW WEIGHT LINE **
2760 REM
2770 COLOR 1
2780 PLOT 3, WPLOT(1)
2790 FOR WEEK = 2 TO 52
2800 IF FLAG(WEEK) = 1 THEN PLOT 3 * WEEK,
WPLOT : GOTO 2820
2810 DRAWTO 3 * WEEK, WPLOT(WEEK)
2820 NEXT WEEK
2830 PRINT "PROGRAM ENDED"
2840 END
```

Section 2

Educational Programs

- State Capital Quiz
- Math Quiz
- Spelling Exerciser
- Pattern Recognition
- English - Metric Converter

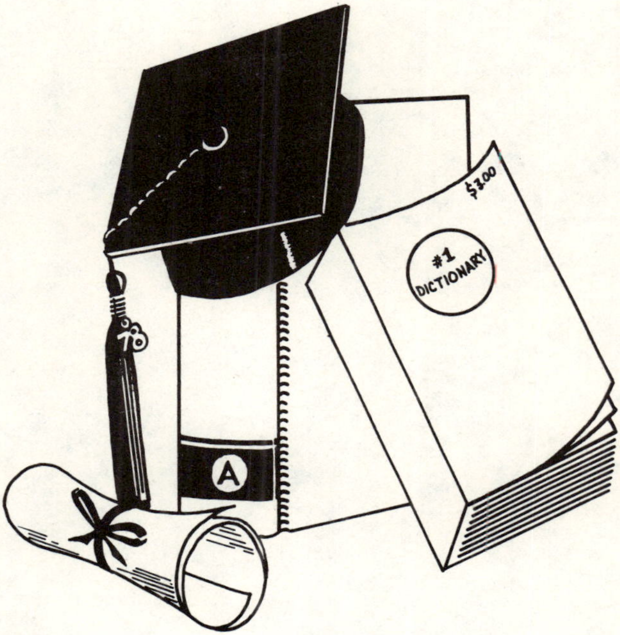

EDUCATIONAL PROGRAMS

The programs in this section are devoted to improving skills in some basic areas of learning. The first program is a quiz to test your ability to memorize state capitals. There is also a math quiz and a spelling quiz. Also included is a program to help develop skills for recognizing numeric patterns. The final program in this section is a Metric conversion program. Although it is not in a quiz form, this program has been included in this section because you can learn about the Metric system by making conversions.

State Capital Quiz

Do you remember the capitals of every state in the union? Use this quiz to find out. The quiz is ideal for elementary school students who want to brush up before an exam. It is also good for older students. If you also want to memorize national capitals, this program can be easily modified. Simply change the DATA statements. Remember to first list the nation, then the capital. Also, the last element of DATA must be 'ZZZ'. Element 'ZZZ' is known as an end of data flag.

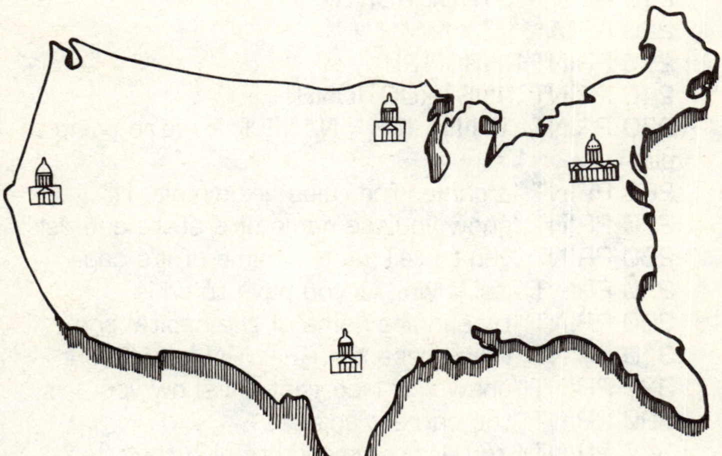

```
10 REM *** STATE CAPITALS ***
20 REM
30 DIM A$(1), STATE$(14), CAP$(14), AN$(14),
NAME$(20)
40 PRINT CHR$(125)
50 PRINT ,"STATE CAPITALS"
60 PRINT : PRINT "What is your name";
70 INPUT NAME$
80 PRINT : PRINT "Do you want to read the
instructions,"
90 PRINT NAME$; " (answer 'Y' or 'N')";
100 INPUT A$
110 IF A$ = "N" THEN 430
120 IF A$ <> "Y" THEN 80
200 REM ****************
210 REM INSTRUCTIONS
220 REM ****************
230 PRINT CHR$(125)
240 PRINT ,"INSTRUCTIONS"
250 PRINT : PRINT "OK"; NAME$; ", we're going to
play"
260 PRINT "a game. The rules are simple. I'll"
270 PRINT "show you the name of a state and ask"
280 PRINT "you to tell me the name of it's cap-"
290 PRINT "ital town. All you have to do is"
300 PRINT "type in the name of the capital and"
310 PRINT "then press the RETURN key. If your"
320 PRINT "answer is incorrect, I'll show you"
330 PRINT "the correct answer."
340 PRINT "You are now ready to play the"
350 PRINT "game. Press the RETURN key and the"
360 PRINT "game will start."
370 PRINT : PRINT "PRESS RETURN TO START";
380 INPUT A$
400 REM *************
410 REM PLAY GAME
420 REM *************
430 RIGHT = 0
```

```
440 TOTAL = 0
450 PRINT CHR$(125)
460 READ STATE$
470 IF STATE$ = "ZZZ" THEN 730
480 READ CAP$
490 PRINT : PRINT "What is the capital of "
500 PRINT STATE$;
510 INPUT AN$
520 IF AN$ <> CAP$ THEN 560
530 RIGHT = RIGHT + 1
540 PRINT CHR$(253) : PRINT "CORRECT, ";
NAME$; "!"
550 GOTO 580
560 PRINT : PRINT "Incorrect. The capital of "
570 PRINT STATE$; " is "; CAP$; "."
580 TOTAL = TOTAL + 1
590 PRINT : PRINT "PRESS SPACE BAR TO
CONTINUE."
600 PRINT : PRINT "PRESS 'RETURN' TO STOP."
610 KEY = PEEK(764)
620 POKE 764, 255
630 IF KEY = 33 THEN 450
640 IF KEY <> 12 THEN 610
700 REM  *******************
710 REM COMPUTE SCORE
720 REM  *******************
730 SCORE = INT(RIGHT / TOTAL * 100)
740 PRINT CHR$(125)
750 PRINT : PRINT "You were right on "; RIGHT;"
out of "; TOTAL
760 PRINT "questions for a score of "; SCORE; "%."
770 IF SCORE = 100 THEN PRINT "Excellent, ";
NAME$; "!" : GOTO 800
780 IF SCORE > 90 THEN PRINT "Very good, ";
NAME$ ; "!"
790 IF SCORE < 80 THEN PRINT "You can use
some more practice."
800 PRINT : PRINT "Do you want to play again (Y or
N)";
```

```
810 INPUT A$
820 IF A$ = "Y" THEN RESTORE :GOTO 430
830 IF A$ <> "N" THEN 800
840 PRINT : PRINT "SEE YOU LATER, "; NAME$;
"!"
850 END
900 REM *****
910 REM DATA
920 REM *****
930 DATA ALABAMA, MONTGOMERY, ALASKA,
JUNEAU, ARIZONA, PHOENIX
940 DATA ARKANSAS, LITTLE ROCK,
CALIFORNIA, SACRAMENTO, COLORADO,
DENVER
950 DATA CONNECTICUT, HARTFORD,
DELAWARE, DOVER, FLORIDA, TALLAHASSEE
960 DATA GEORGIA, ATLANTA, HAWAII,
HONOLULU, IDAHO, BOISE, ILLINOIS,
SPRINGFIELD
970 DATA INDIANA, INDIANAPOLIS, IOWA, DES
MOINES, KANSAS, TOPEKA
980 DATA KENTUCKY, FRANKFORT, LOUISIANA,
BATON ROUGE, MAINE, AUGUSTA
990 DATA MARYLAND, ANNAPOLIS,
MASSACHUSETTS, BOSTON, MICHIGAN,
LANSING
1000 DATA MINNESOTA, ST. PAUL, MISSISSIPPI,
JACKSON, MISSOURI, JEFFERSON CITY
1010 DATA MONTANA, HELENA, NEBRASKA,
LINCOLN, NEVADA, CARSON CITY
1020 DATA NEW HAMPSHIRE, CONCORD, NEW
JERSEY, TRENTON, NEW MEXICO, SANTA FE
1030 DATA NEW YORK, ALBANY, NORTH
CAROLINA, RALEIGH, NORTH DAKOTA,
BISMARCK
1040 DATA OHIO, COLUMBUS, OKLAHOMA,
OKLAHOMA CITY, OREGON, SALEM
1050 DATA PENNSYLVANIA, HARRISBURG,
```

```
RHODE ISLAND, PROVIDENCE
1060 DATA SOUTH CAROLINA, COLUMBIA,
SOUTH DAKOTA, PIERRE, TENNESSEE,
NASHVILLE
1070 DATA TEXAS, AUSTIN, UTAH, SALT LAKE
CITY, VERMONT, MONTPELIER
1080 DATA VIRGINIA, RICHMOND, WASHINGTON,
OLYMPIA, WEST VIRGINIA, CHARLESTON
1090 DATA WISCONSIN, MADISON, WYOMING,
CHEYENNE, ZZZ
```

Math Quiz

Here's a math quiz for elementary school children learning the basics. The program randomly selects problems in addition, subtraction, multiplication, and division. You are given one minute to answer each question. At the end of the quiz, the program will score your performance. The program awards bonus points if you correctly answer a problem quickly. However, you score more for accuracy than speed.

The program also has a feature that allows you to review the problems you've missed. The program does this by converting each wrong answer to the string variable ELEM$ (lines 1540–1780). At line 1790 the program concatenates each wrong answer into the string WRONG$. The string is split and printed in lines 2130 - 2190.

```
10 REM *** MATH QUIZ ***
20 REM
30 GRAPHICS 0
40 DIM A$(1), N$(12), X$(3), Y$(2), Z$(3)
50 DIM ELEM$(13), OP$(1), WRONG$(130)
60 DIM SCORE(100)
70 N = 0
80 PRINT CHR$(125)
90 PRINT ,"MATH GAME"
100 PRINT : PRINT "What is your name";
110 INPUT N$
120 PRINT CHR$(125)
130 PRINT : PRINT "Hello, "; N$; "!"
140 PRINT : PRINT "Do you want to see the
instructions"
150 PRINT "(answer Y or N)";
160 INPUT A$
170 IF A$ = "N" THEN PRINT CHR$(125) : GOTO 390
180 IF A$ <> "Y" THEN 140
200 REM ****************
210 REM INSTRUCTIONS
220 REM ****************
230 PRINT CHR$(125)
240 PRINT : PRINT ,"INSTRUCTIONS"
250 PRINT : PRINT " OK "; N$; ". We're going to"
260 PRINT "play a game. The rules are easy. I"
270 PRINT "will show you a math problem. When"
280 PRINT "you see the problem, I want you to"
290 PRINT "type in the answer and then press"
300 PRINT "the RETURN key. I will give you one"
310 PRINT "minute to answer the problem. If you"
320 PRINT "can't answer the problem in one min-"
330 PRINT "ute, I will give you another problem."
340 PRINT "Each time we play the game I will"
350 PRINT "give you 10 problems. At the end of"
360 PRINT "the game I will tell you how well"
370 PRINT "you have done. That's all there is"
380 PRINT "to it!"
```

```
390 PRINT : PRINT "WHEN YOU ARE READY TO
PLAY THE GAME"
400 PRINT "JUST PRESS THE RETURN KEY."
410 INPUT A$
500 REM *****************
510 REM SET VARIABLES
520 REM *****************
530 N = N + 1
540 NUM = 0
550 WRONG = 0
560 FLAG = 0
570 J = 1
580 LN = 13
590 SCORE = 0
600 FOR I = 1 TO 100
610 WRONG$(I,I) = " "
620 NEXT I
630 GRAPHICS 2
640 SETCOLOR 4, 10, 10
650 SETCOLOR 0, 8, 8
700 REM ***********************
710 REM GENERATE PROBLEM
720 REM ***********************
730 PRINT CHR$(125)
740 NUM = NUM + 1
750 PROB = INT(4 * RND(0) + 1)
760 A = INT(12 * RND(0)) + 1
770 B = INT(12 * RND(0)) + 1
780 POSITION 8, 0
790 PRINT #6; "1:00"
800 POSITION 7, 5
810 ON PROB GOTO 850, 920, 1000, 1070
820 REM
830 REM ** ADDITION **
840 REM
850 CORR = A + B
860 PRINT #6; A; "+"; B; "= ? "
870 OP$ = "+"
```

```
880 GOTO 1230
890 REM
900 REM ** SUBTRACTION **
910 REM
920 IF A - B < 0 THEN 760
930 CORR = A - B
940 PRINT #6; A; "-"; B; "=? "
950 OP$ = "-"
960 GOTO 1230
970 REM
980 REM **MULTIPLICATION **
990 REM
1000 CORR = A * B
1010 PRINT #6; A; "×"; B; "= ? "
1020 OP$ = "×"
1030 GOTO 1230
1040 REM
1050 REM ** DIVISION **
1060 REM
1070 C = A * B
1080 CORR = B
1090 PRINT #6; C; "/"; A; "=? "
1100 OP$ = "/"
1200 REM ********************
1210 REM ANSWER PROBLEM
1220 REM ********************
1230 CLOCK = 60
1240 FOR TIME = 1 TO 75
1250 K = PEEK(764)
1260 TRAP 1280
1270 IF K <> 255 THEN INPUT ANS : GOTO 1430
1280 NEXT TIME
1290 POSITION 8, 0
1300 CLOCK = CLOCK - 1
1310 IF CLOCK <= 9 THEN 1340
1320 PRINT #6; "0"; CLOCK
1330 GOTO 1240
```

```
1340 PRINT #6; "0:0"; CLOCK
1350 IF CLOCK = 0 THEN PRINT CHR$(253) :
ANS = -1 : GOTO 1430
1360 GOTO 1240
1400 REM *******************
1410 REM CHECK PROBLEM
1420 REM *******************
1430 IF ANS <> CORR AND NUM < 10 THEN
1530
1440 IF ANS <> CORR THEN FLAG = 1 : GOTO
1530
1450 SCORE = SCORE + 10
1460 IF CLOCK > 40 THEN SCORE = SCORE + 1
1470 IF CLOCK > 50 THEN SCORE = SCORE + 1
1480 IF NUM < 10 THEN 730
1490 GOTO 1930
1500 REM **************************
1510 REM SAVE WRONG ANSWER
1520 REM **************************
1530 WRONG = WRONG + 1
1540 IF PROB = 4 THEN X$ = STR$(C)
1550 IF PROB = 4 THEN Y$ = STR$(A) : GOTO
1580
1560 X$ = STR$(A)
1570 Y$ = STR$(B)
1580 Z$ = STR$(CORR)
1590 FOR N = 1 TO 13
1600 ELEM$(N,N) = " "
1610 NEXT N
1620 I = 1
1630 L = LEN(X$) - 1
1640 ELEM$(I,I + L) = X$
1650 I = I + L + 1
1660 ELEM$(I,I) = " "
1670 I = I + 1
1680 ELEM$(I,I) = OP$
1690 I = I + 1
1700 ELEM$(I,I) = " "
```

```
1710 I = I + 1
1720 L = LEN(Y$) - 1
1730 ELEM$(I,I + L) = Y$
1740 I = I + L + 1
1750 ELEM$(I,I + 2) = " = "
1760 I = I + 3
1770 L = LEN(Z$) - 1
1780 ELEM$(I,I + L) = Z$
1790 WRONG$(J,J + LN - 1) = ELEM$
1800 J = J + LN
1810 IF FLAG = 1 THEN 1930
1820 GOTO 730
1900 REM ***************
1910 REM FINISH GAME
1920 REM ***************
1930 SCORE(N) = SCORE
1940 GRAPHICS 0
1950 PRINT CHR$(125)
1960 PRINT : PRINT "You have finished the game, ";
N$; "."
1970 PRINT "Good for you!"
1980 PRINT : PRINT "Your score is "; SCORE;
"points."
1990 IF SCORE >= 100 THEN PRINT
"Outstanding, "; N$; "!" : GOTO 2010
2000 IF SCORE >= 80 THEN PRINT "Good score,
"; N$; "."
2010 IF WRONG = 0 THEN 2200
2020 PRINT : PRINT "Do you want to see the
problem";
2030 IF WRONG > 1 then print "s";
2040 PRINT " YOU"
2050 PRINT "MISSED";
2060 INPUT A$
2070 IF A$ = "N" THEN 2200
2080 IF A$ <> "Y" THEN 2020
2100 REM ******************************
2110 REM DISPLAY WRONG ANSWERS
2120 REM ******************************
```

```
2130 PRINT CHR$(125)
2140 J = 1
2150 FOR I = 1 TO WRONG
2160 PRINT WRONG$(J,J + LN - 1)
2170 PRINT
2180 J = J + LN
2190 NEXT I
2200 PRINT : PRINT "Do you want to play again
(answer Y"
2210 PRINT "or N)";
2220 INPUT A$
2230 IF A$ = "Y" THEN PRINT CHR$(125) : GOTO
530
2240 IF A$ <> "N" THEN 2200
2250 PRINT : PRINT "So long, "; N$; ". See you
later!"
2260 END
```

Spelling Exerciser

The following program can be used to strengthen your power of recall and spelling. The program is a game that flashes words on the video screen. Your response is to correctly spell the word you have seen. The program offers three speeds. The higher the speed, the less amount of time you will have to read the words.

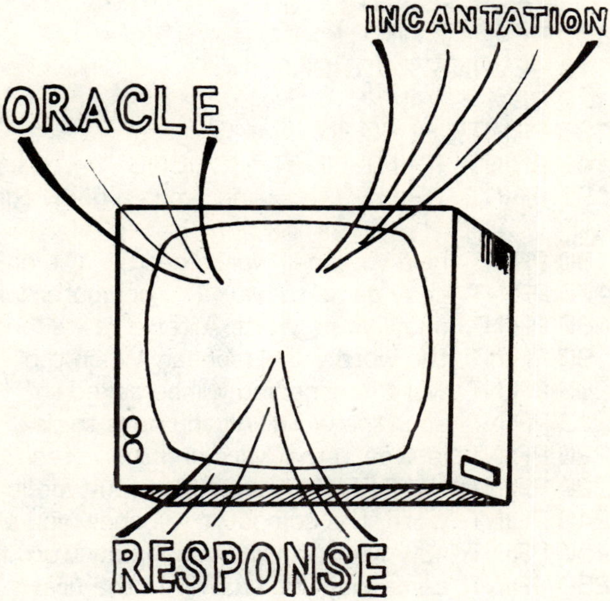

You can adjust the speeds by changing the values for the variable SPEED in lines 610 - 630. You can also change the words used by the program by adding your own with DATA statements such as the one in line 1230. You can use as many words as you like. The last item in the DATA statements must be 'ZZZ'. This signals an end of data. Also, if one of your words exceeds 15 characters, change the DIMensions of WORD$ and REPLY$ in line 30.

```
10 REM *** SPELLING EXERCISER ***
20 REM
30 DIM A$(1), N$(12), REPLY$(15), WORD$(15)
40 PRINT CHR$(125)
50 PRINT : PRINT "Do you want to read the
instructions"
60 PRINT "(answer Y or N)";
70 INPUT A$
80 IF A$ = "N" THEN 430
90 IF A$ <> "Y" THEN 60
100 REM ****************
110 REM INSTRUCTIONS
120 REM ****************
130 PRINT CHR$(125)
140 PRINT : PRINT ,"INSTRUCTIONS"
150 PRINT : PRINT " This program is a game that
will"
160 PRINT "help you spell words better. It is an"
170 PRINT "easy game to play. The computer will"
180 PRINT "show you a word. After a few seconds"
190 PRINT "the word will disappear. When the"
200 PRINT "word is gone you will be asked to"
210 PRINT "spell the word. All you have to do"
220 PRINT "is type in the word and then press"
230 PRINT "the RETURN key. After you type in the"
240 PRINT "word, the computer will show you a"
250 PRINT "new word. Answer each new word the"
260 PRINT "same way you answered the first
word."
270 PRINT : PRINT "AFTER YOU READ THESE
INSTRUCTIONS"
280 PRINT "YOU WILL BE READY TO PLAY THE
GAME."
290 PRINT "IF YOU ARE READY, PRESS THE
RETURN KEY";
300 INPUT A$
400 REM ***************
410 REM PLAYER INPUT
420 REM ***************
```

```
430 PRINT CHR$(125)
440 PRINT : PRINT "What is your name";
450 INPUT N$
460 TOTAL = 0
470 RIGHT = 0
480 PRINT : PRINT "OK "; N$; "one more thing
before"
490 PRINT "we can start. Choose one of the three"
500 PRINT "speeds below. If you choose FAST the"
510 PRINT "word will disappear after a short"
520 PRINT "time. If you choose SLOW the word"
530 PRINT "will disappear after a longer amount"
540 PRINT "of time."
550 PRINT : PRINT "What speed do you want?"
560 PRINT : PRINT "1) FAST 2) MEDIUM 3) SLOW";
570 TRAP 560
580 INPUT SPEED
590 IF SPEED < 1 OR SPEED > 3 THEN 560
600 ON SPEED GOTO 610, 620, 630
610 SPEED = 30 : GOTO 640
620 SPEED = 60 : GOTO 640
630 SPEED = 90
640 PRINT : PRINT "OK "; N$; ", you are now ready"
650 PRINT "to begin the game. When you want to"
660 PRINT "start press the RETURN key";
670 INPUT A$
700 REM ************
710 REM RUN GAME
720 REM ************
730 PRINT CHR$(125)
740 READ WORD$
750 IF WORD$ = "ZZZ" THEN 930
760 TOTAL = TOTAL+1
770 PRINT : PRINT ,WORD$
780 FOR TIME = 1 TO SPEED
790 NEXT TIME
800 PRINT CHR$(125) : REM ** WORD
DISAPPEARS **
```

```
810 PRINT : PRINT "Spell the word."
820 INPUT REPLY$
830 IF REPLY$ = WORD$ THEN PRINT : PRINT
CHR$(253) : PRINT "CORRECT!"
840 IF REPLY$ = WORD$ THEN RIGHT = RIGHT
+ 1 : GOTO 860
850 PRINT : PRINT "INCORRECT."
860 PRINT : PRINT "When you are ready for the
next word"
870 PRINT "press the RETURN key.";
880 INPUT A$
890 GOTO 730
900 REM ***************
910 REM END OF GAME
920 REM ***************
930 PRINT CHR$(125)
940 PERCENT = RIGHT / TOTAL * 100
950 PRINT : PRINT " You have finished the game.
You"
960 PRINT "were correct on "; RIGHT; " out of ";
TOTAL; " words for"
970 PRINT " a score of "; PERCENT; " percent."
980 IF PERCENT >= 80 THEN PRINT " Very good,
"; N$; "!" : GOTO 1020
990 PRINT " Maybe you should play with these"
1000 PRINT "words some more before trying any
new"
1010 PRINT "ones,"; N$; "."
1020 PRINT : PRINT " Do you want to play the
game"
1030 PRINT "again, "; N$; "?"
1040 PRINT :PRINT "IF YOU WANT TO PLAY
AGAIN, TYPE"
1050 PRINT "the Y key and then press RETURN."
1060 PRINT " If you do not want to play, type"
1070 PRINT "the N key and then press RETURN."
1080 INPUT A$
1090 IF A$ = "N" THEN PRINT : PRINT " Bye, ";
```

```
N$; ". See you later!" : END
1100 IF A$ <> "Y" THEN 1040
1110 RESTORE
1120 PRINT CHR$(125)
1130 GOTO 460
1200 REM *****
1210 REM DATA
1220 REM *****
1230 DATA DOG, CAT, MOUSE, BIRD, ZZZ
```

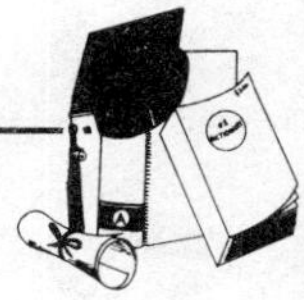

Pattern Recognition

This is a game that will test and improve your ability to recognize simple numeric patterns. First, the program randomly selects the type of pattern (line 430). There are seven different patterns. Next, the program randomly generates the numbers in the series (lines 530 - 1400). The fifth number in a series is assigned to the numeric variable ANS. If your answer corresponds to this variable, you have answered the problem correctly. As a programming exercise you can expand the number of patterns (or better yet, create the patterns randomly).

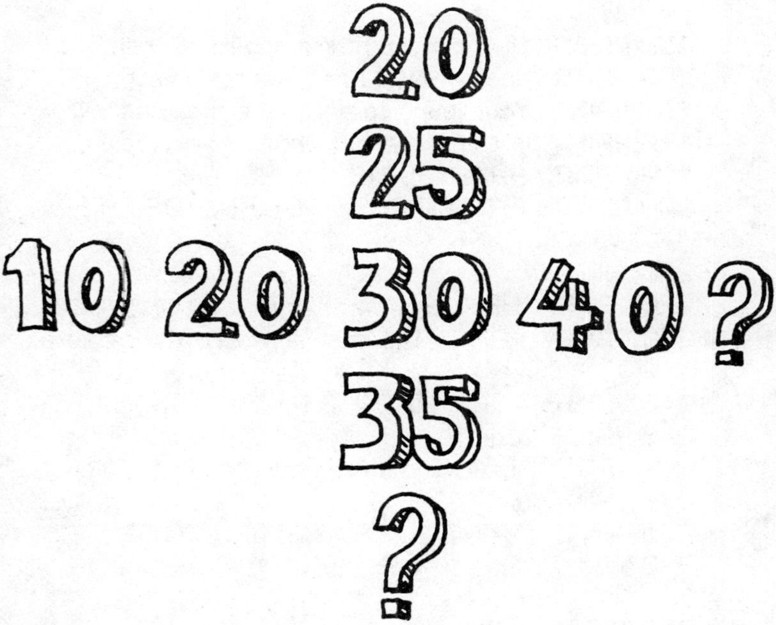

```
10 REM *** PATTERN RECOGNITION ***
20 REM
30 DIM A$(1), REPLY$(3)
40 PRINT CHR$(125)
50 PRINT ,"PATTERNS"
60 PRINT : PRINT "Do you want instructions (Y or
N)";
70 INPUT A$
80 IF A$ = "N" THEN 300
90 IF A$ <> "Y" THEN 60
100 REM  ***************
110 REM INSTRUCTIONS
120 REM  ***************
130 PRINT CHR$(125)
140 PRINT : PRINT "OK here's how the game is
played."
150 PRINT "I'll show you four numbers. These four"
160 PRINT "numbers will form a certain pattern."
170 PRINT "Your job is to enter the fifth number"
180 PRINT "in the pattern. Here is an example:"
190 PRINT : PRINT " 5, 10, 15, 20, ?"
200 PRINT : PRINT "PRESS RETURN FOR THE
ANSWER"
210 INPUT A$
220 PRINT CHR$(125)
230 PRINT : PRINT "The answer is 25. The pattern
is"
240 PRINT "5, 10, 15, 20, 25. When you want to"
250 PRINT "stop playing, type in 'Q' for your"
260 PRINT "answer. You are now ready to begin"
270 PRINT "play."
280 PRINT : PRINT "PRESS RETURN TO START";
290 INPUT A$
300 RIGHT = 0
310 TOTAL = 0
400 REM  ******************
410 REM CHOOSE PATTERN
420 REM  ******************
```

```
430 PATT = INT(7 * RND(0)) + 1
440 IF PATT = 4 THEN FLAG = 1
450 ON PATT GOTO 500, 600, 700, 700, 1000,
1100, 1300
500 REM ************
510 REM PATTERN 1
520 REM ************
530 NUM = INT(10 * RND(0)) + 1
540 A1 = NUM
550 A2 = 2 * NUM
560 A3 = 3 * NUM
570 A4 = 4 * NUM
580 ANS = 5 * NUM
590 GOTO 1500
600 REM ************
610 REM PATTERN 2
620 REM ************
630 NUM = INT(9 * RND(0)) + 1
640 A1 = NUM
650 A2 = 2 * NUM
660 A3 = 2 * A2
670 A4 = 2 * A3
680 ANS = 2 * A4
690 GOTO 1500
700 REM ************
710 REM PATTERN 3
720 REM ************
730 NUM = INT(10 * RND(0)) + 1
740 A1 = INT(NUM ^ 2 + 0.1)
750 A2 = INT((NUM + 1) ^ 2 + 0.1)
760 A3 = INT((NUM + 2) ^ 2 + 0.1)
770 A4 = INT((NUM + 3) ^ 2 + 0.1)
780 ANS = INT((NUM + 4) ^ 2 + 0.1)
790 IF FLAG = 1 THEN 810
800 GOTO 1500
810 TEMP1 = A1
820 TEMP2 = A2
830 TEMP4 = A4
```

```
840 TEMP5 = ANS
900 REM ************
910 REM PATTERN 4
920 REM ************
930 A1 = TEMP5
940 A2 = TEMP4
950 A4 = TEMP2
960 ANS = TEMP1
970 FLAG = 0
980 GOTO 1500
1000 REM ************
1010 REM PATTERN 5
1020 REM ************
1030 NUM = INT(10 * RND(0)) + 1
1040 A1 = INT(100 * RND(0)) + 1
1050 A2 = A1 - NUM
1060 A3 = A2 - NUM
1070 A4 = A3 - NUM
1080 ANS = A4 - NUM
1090 GOTO 1500
1100 REM ************
1110 REM PATTERN 6
1120 REM ************
1130 NUM1 = INT(10 * RND(0)) + 1
1140 NUM2 = INT(10 * RND(0)) + 1
1150 IF NUM1 = NUM2 THEN 1330
1160 A1 = INT(100 * RND(0)) + 1
1170 A2 = A1 - NUM1
1180 A3 = A2 + NUM2
1190 A4 = A3 - NUM1
1200 ANS = A4 + NUM2
1210 GOTO 1500
1300 REM ************
1310 REM PATTERN 7
1320 REM ************
1330 NUM1 = INT(10 * RND(0)) + 1
1340 NUM2 = INT(10 * RND(0)) + 1
1350 IF NUM1 = NUM2 THEN 1130
```

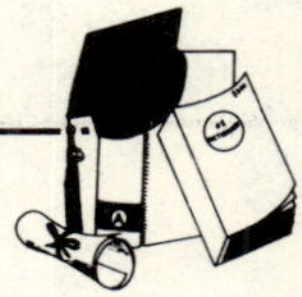

```
1360 A1 = INT(100 * RND(0)) + 1
1370 A2 = A1 + NUM1
1380 A3 = A2 - NUM2
1390 A4 = A3 + NUM1
1400 ANS = A4 - NUM2
1500 REM  *************
1510 REM USER INPUT
1520 REM  *************
1530 PRINT CHR$(125)
1540 PRINT : PRINT A1; ", "; A2; ", "; A3; ", "; A4; ",
";
1560 INPUT REPLY$
1570 IF REPLY$ = "Q" THEN 1800
1580 TRAP 1540
1590 IF VAL(REPLY$) = ANS THEN 1660
1600 PRINT : PRINT "INCORRECT. THE CORRECT
NUMBER IS ";ANS
1610 TOTAL = TOTAL + 1
1620 PRINT : PRINT A1; ", "; A2; ", "; A3; ", "; A4; ",
"; ANS
1630 PRINT : PRINT "PRESS RETURN FOR NEXT
PATTERN";
1640 INPUT A$
1650 GOTO 430
1660 PRINT CHR$(253);
1670 PRINT : PRINT "CORRECT!"
1680 RIGHT = RIGHT + 1
1690 TOTAL = TOTAL + 1
1700 PRINT : PRINT A1; ", "; A2; ", "; A3; ", "; A4;
","; ANS
1710 PRINT : PRINT "PRESS RETURN FOR NEXT
PATTERN";
1720 INPUT A$
1730 GOTO 430
1800 REM  ********************
1810 REM CALCULATE SCORE
1820 REM  ********************
1830 PRINT CHR$(125)
```

```
1840 SCORE = INT(RIGHT / TOTAL * 100)
1850 PRINT : PRINT "You were correct on ";
RIGHT;" OUT OF"
1860 PRINT TOTAL;" patterns for a score of";
SCORE; "%."
1870 PRINT : PRINT "Play again (Y or N)";
1880 INPUT A$
1890 IF A$ = "Y" THEN 290
1900 IF A$ <> "N" THEN 1870
1910 PRINT : PRINT "PROGRAM ENDED."
1920 END
```

English - Metric Converter

This program converts from English to Metric and vice versa. The program converts the commonly used units of length, weight capacity, and temperature. When RUN, the program displays a main menu. Select one of the five options and press RETURN.

Next, the program displays a menu with the English and Metric units to be converted. You will notice the prompt "CONVERT FROM?" Input the menu number of the unit you are converting from. Now the program prompts "CONVERT TO?" Input the menu number of the unit you want to convert to. The program will ask "INPUT NUMBER OF UNITS?" Input the amount of whatever it is you're converting from. The program will display the answer. At this point you have two options: press the SPACE BAR and the menu you are currently in will remain for you to make another conversion or press RETURN and you will return to the main menu.

```
10 REM *** METRIC CONVERTER ***
20 REM
30 DIM A$(1), UNIT1$(11), UNIT2$(11)
100 REM *************
110 REM MAIN MENU
120 REM *************
130 PRINT CHR$(125)
140 PRINT : PRINT " 1) LENGTH"
150 PRINT : PRINT " 2) WEIGHT"
160 PRINT : PRINT " 3) CAPACITY"
170 PRINT : PRINT " 4) TEMPERATURE"
180 PRINT : PRINT " 5) END PROGRAM"
190 PRINT : PRINT "SELECT OPTION";
200 TRAP 190
210 INPUT N
220 IF N < 1 OR N > 5 THEN 190
230 ON N GOTO 330, 1130, 1730, 2330, 240
240 PRINT : PRINT "PROGRAM ENDED."
250 END
300 REM **********
310 REM LENGTH
320 REM **********
330 PRINT CHR$(125)
340 PRINT : PRINT " 1) INCHES", "5)
MILLIMETERS"
350 PRINT : PRINT " 2) FEET ", "6) CENTIMETERS"
360 PRINT : PRINT " 3) YARDS", "7)
DECIMETERS"
370 PRINT : PRINT " 4) MILES", "8) METERS"
380 PRINT : PRINT ,, " 9) KILOMETERS"
390 PRINT : PRINT "CONVERT FROM";
400 TRAP 390
410 INPUT F
420 IF F < 1 OR F > 9 THEN 390
430 PRINT : PRINT "CONVERT TO";
440 TRAP 430
450 INPUT T
460 IF F < 5 AND T < 5 THEN 430
```

```
470 IF F > 5 AND T >5 THEN 430
480 IF T < 1 OR T > 9 THEN 430
490 IF F < 5 THEN ON F GOTO 510, 540, 570,
600
500 IF F > 5 THEN ON F - 4 GOTO 630, 660,
690, 720, 750
510 C = 25.4
520 UNIT1$ = "INCHES"
530 GOTO 770
540 C = 304.8
550 UNIT1$ = "FEET"
560 GOTO 770
570 C = 914.4
580 UNIT1$ = "YARDS"
590 GOTO 770
600 C = 1609304
610 UNIT1$ = "MILES"
620 GOTO 770
630 C = 3.3E - 03
640 UNIT1$ = "MILLIMETERS"
650 GOTO 770
660 C = 0.0328
670 UNIT1$ = "CENTIMETERS"
680 GOTO 770
690 C = 0.3281
700 UNIT1$ = "DECIMETERS"
710 GOTO 770
720 C = 3.2808
730 UNIT1$ = "METERS"
740 GOTO 770
750 C = 3280.8315
760 UNIT1$ = "KILOMETERS"
770 IF T < 5 THEN ON T GOTO 790, 820, 850,
880
780 ON T - 4 GOTO 910, 940, 970, 1000, 1030
790 A = 12
800 UNIT2$ = "INCHES"
810 GOTO 2630
```

```
820 A = 1
830 UNIT2$ = "FEET"
840 GOTO 2630
850 A = 0.3333
860 UNIT2$ = "YARDS"
870 GOTO 2630
880 A = 1.894E -04
890 UNIT2$ = "MILES"
900 GOTO 2630
910 A = 1
920 UNIT2$ = "MILLIMETERS"
930 GOTO 2630
940 A = 0.1
950 UNIT2$ = "CENTIMETERS"
960 GOTO 2630
970 A = 0.01
980 UNIT2$ = "DECIMETERS"
990 GOTO 2630
1000 A = 1.0E - 03
1010 UNIT2$ = "METERS"
1020 GOTO 2630
1030 A = 1E - 06
1040 UNIT2$ = "KILOMETERS"
1050 GOTO 2630
1100 REM *********
1110 REM WEIGHT
1120 REM *********
1130 PRINT CHR$(125)
1140 PRINT : PRINT " 1) OUNCES", "4) GRAMS"
1150 PRINT : PRINT " 2) POUNDS", "5)
KILOGRAMS"
1160 PRINT : PRINT " 3) TONS ", "6) METRIC
TONS"
1170 PRINT : PRINT "CONVERT FROM";
1180 TRAP 1170
1190 INPUT F
1200 IF F < 1 OR F > 6 THEN 1170
1210 PRINT : PRINT "CONVERT TO";
```

```
1220 TRAP 1210
1230 INPUT T
1240 IF F < 4 AND T < 4 THEN 1210
1250 IF F >= 4 AND T >= 4 THEN 1210
1260 IF T < 1 OR T > 6 THEN 1210
1270 IF F < 4 THEN ON F GOTO 1290, 1320, 1350
1280 ON F - 3 GOTO 1380, 1410, 1440
1290 C = 28.35
1300 UNIT1$ = "OUNCES"
1310 GOTO 1460
1320 C = 453.6
1330 UNIT1$ = "POUNDS"
1340 GOTO 1460
1350 C = 907200
1360 UNIT1$ = "TONS"
1370 GOTO 1460
1380 C = 2.1875E - 03
1390 UNIT1$ = "GRAMS"
1400 GOTO 1460
1410 C = 2.1875
1420 UNIT1$ = "KILOGRAMS"
1430 GOTO 1460
1440 C = 2204
1450 UNIT1$ = "METRIC TONS"
1460 IF T < 4 THEN ON T GOTO 1480, 1510, 1540
1470 ON T - 3 GOTO 1570, 1600, 1630
1480 A = 16
1490 UNIT2$ = "OUNCES"
1500 GOTO 2630
1510 A = 1
1520 UNIT2$ = "POUNDS"
1530 GOTO 2630
1540 A = 5E - 04
1550 UNIT2$ = "TONS"
1560 GOTO 2630
1570 A = 1
1580 UNIT2$ = "GRAMS"
1590 GOTO 2630
```

```
1600 A = 1.0E - 03
1610 UNIT2$ = "KILOGRAMS"
1620 GOTO 2630
1630 A = 1.00026E - 06
1640 UNIT2$ = "METRIC TONS"
1650 GOTO 2630
1700 REM **********
1710 REM CAPACITY
1720 REM **********
1730 PRINT CHR$(125)
1740 PRINT : PRINT " 1) PINTS ", "5)
MILLILITERS"
1750 PRINT : PRINT " 2) QUARTS", "6) LITERS"
1760 PRINT : PRINT " 3) GALLONS"
1770 PRINT : PRINT " 4) DRY QUARTS"
1780 PRINT : PRINT "CONVERT FROM";
1790 TRAP 1780
1800 INPUT F
1810 IF F < 1 OR F > 6 THEN 1780
1820 PRINT : PRINT "CONVERT TO";
1830 TRAP 1820
1840 INPUT T
1850 IF F < 5 AND T < 5 THEN 1820
1860 IF F >= 5 AND T >= 5 THEN 1820
1870 IF T < 1 OR T > 6 THEN 1820
1880 IF F < 5 THEN ON F GOTO 1900, 1930,
1960, 1990
1890 ON F - 4 GOTO 2020, 2050
1900 C = 0.425
1910 UNIT1$ = "PINTS"
1920 GOTO 2070
1930 C = 0.95
1940 UNIT1$ = "QUARTS"
1950 GOTO 2070
1960 C = 1.9
1970 UNIT1$ = "GALLONS"
1980 GOTO 2070
1990 C = 1.1
```

```
2000 UNIT1$ = "DRY QUARTS"
2010 GOTO 2070
2020 C = 1.06E - 03
2030 UNIT1$ = "MILLILITERS"
2040 GOTO 2070
2050 C = 1.06
2060 UNIT1$ = "LITERS"
2070 IF T < 5 THEN ON T GOTO 2090, 2120,
2150, 2180
2080 ON T - 4 GOTO 2210, 2240
2090 A = 2
2100 UNIT2$ = "PINTS"
2110 GOTO 2630
2120 A = 1
2130 UNIT2$ = "QUARTS"
2140 GOTO 2630
2150 A = 0.5
2160 UNIT2$ = "GALLONS"
2170 GOTO 2630
2180 A = 0.859
2190 UNIT2$ = "DRY QUARTS"
2200 GOTO 2630
2210 A = 1000
2220 UNIT2$ = "MILLILITERS"
2230 GOTO 2630
2240 A = 1
2250 UNIT2$ = "LITERS"
2260 GOTO 2630
2300 REM ****************
2310 REM TEMPERATURE
2320 REM ****************
2330 PRINT CHR$(125)
2340 PRINT : PRINT " 1) FAHRENHEIT", "2)
CENTIGRADE"
2350 PRINT : PRINT "CONVERT FROM";
2360 TRAP 2350
2370 INPUT F
2380 IF F < 1 OR F > 2 THEN 2350
```

```
2390 ON F GOTO 2400, 2430
2400 UNIT1$ = "FAHRENHEIT"
2410 UNIT2$ = "CENTIGRADE"
2420 GOTO 2450
2430 UNIT1$ = "CENTIGRADE"
2440 UNIT2$ = "FAHRENHEIT"
2450 PRINT : PRINT "INPUT DEGREES "; UNIT1$;
2460 TRAP 2450
2470 INPUT NUM
2480 IF F = 1 THEN ANS = (NUM - 32) * 5 / 9
2490 IF F = 2 THEN ANS = NUM * 9 / 5 + 32
2500 PRINT : PRINT NUM; " DEGREES ";
UNIT1$(1,1); " = "; ANS; " DEGREES ";
UNIT2$(1,1)
2510 GOTO 2690
2600 REM **********************
2610 REM CONVERT, ANSWER
2620 REM **********************
2630 PRINT : PRINT "INPUT NUMBER OF ";
UNIT1$;
2640 TRAP 2630
2650 INPUT NUM
2660 IF NUM <= 0 THEN 2630
2670 ANS = NUM * C * A
2680 PRINT : PRINT NUM; " "; UNIT1$; " = "; ANS;
" "; UNIT2$
2690 KEY = PEEK(764)
2700 POKE 764, 255
2710 IF KEY = 12 THEN 130
2720 IF KEY = 33 THEN ON N GOTO 330, 1130,
1730, 2330
2730 GOTO 2690
```

Section 3

Programs for Entertainment

- Number Guess
- Joystick Doodler
- Craps Game
- Role - Playing Dice Roller
- Role - Playing Character Generator

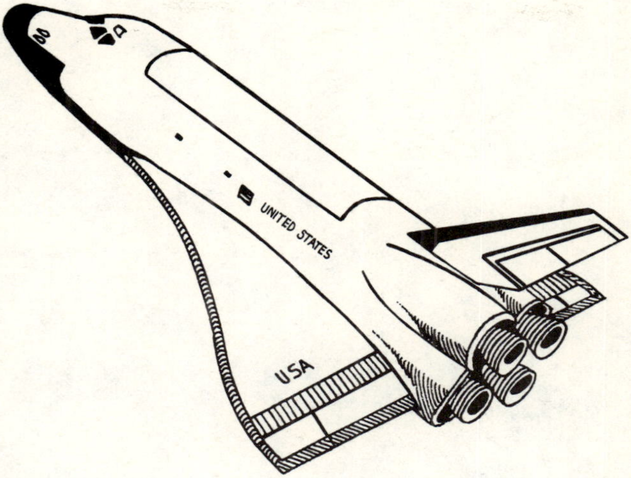

ENTERTAINMENT

The programs in this part of the book will give you an idea of the types of game applications possible on your Atari. The first game is a simple number guessing game, the second game is a program that enables you to draw pictures on your monitor using a joystick. The next game is Craps, this game introduces you to the interesting area of simulations. The final two games are actually game aids. With the increasing popularity of Fantasy / Sci - Fi role playing games, it seems appropriate to use your Atari to lessen the paper work involved with these games. The role playing Dice Roller is very helpful in the middle of a game when you have to roll large numbers of dice to resolve combat and damage. With the Character Generator you can create literally thousands of characters by simply entering a few numbers. The nice feature of this program is it's adaptable to any role playing system.

Number Guess

One of the first programs most people write is a number guessing game. If you haven't done one, here it is!

In line 340, the program generates a random number between 1 and 100. Lines 360 - 400 input your guess. If you're wondering what line 390 (TRAP 380) means, this line is an error trap. If by accident you entered a letter instead of a number in response to line 380, an ERROR- 8 (INPUT Statement Type Mismatch) would occur and the program would end. What the TRAP does is tell the computer that if an error occurs, go to line 380 rather than end the program.

Lines 420 - 440 compares your guess (GUESS) with the random number (N). The variable T is a counter that counts the number of guesses you make.

```
10 REM *** NUMBER GUESS ***
20 REM
30 DIM A$(1)
40 PRINT CHR$(125)
100 REM ****************
110 REM INSTRUCTIONS
120 REM ****************
130 PRINT : PRINT "I will choose a number from 1
to 100."
140 PRINT "Try to guess the number. I will give"
150 PRINT "you hints as you guess. When you are"
160 PRINT "ready to play press the RETURN key."
170 INPUT A$
300 REM *************
310 REM PLAY GAME
320 REM *************
330 PRINT CHR$(125)
340 N = INT(100 * RND(0)) + 1
350 T = 0
360 PRINT : PRINT "I am thinking of a number
between 1"
370 PRINT "and 100."
380 PRINT : PRINT "GUESS MY NUMBER";
390 TRAP 380
400 INPUT GUESS
410 T = T + 1
420 IF GUESS < N THEN PRINT : PRINT "Too low,
try a higher number.":GOTO 380
430 IF GUESS > N THEN PRINT : PRINT "Too high,
try a lower number." : GOTO 380
440 IF GUESS = N THEN PRINT : PRINT "YOU
GUESSED MY NUMBER!"
450 PRINT : PRINT "You guessed the number in " ; T
; " tries."
460 PRINT : PRINT " Want to play again (answer
Y or N)";
470 INPUT A$
480 IF A$ = "Y" THEN 330
```

```
490 IF A$ <> "N" THEN 460
500 PRINT : PRINT "BYE!"
510 END
```

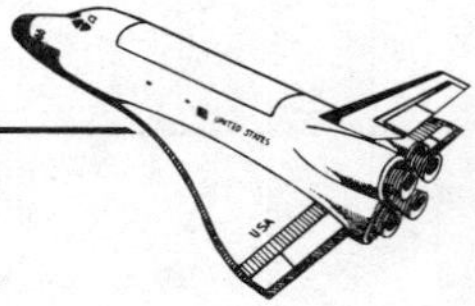

Joystick Doodler

With this program and a joystick you can use your Atari as a doodler. Young children will really enjoy this program. After you insert your joystick and press RETURN the program will ask you to input the starting X and Y coordinates. This will determine the starting position of your "brush." You will have the following options: 1) use the joystick to draw, 2) press the SPACE BAR to turn off the "brush" - you can keep track of the brush movement by watching the coordinate display at the bottom left of the screen, 3) press the FIRE button to erase the screen and start over, 4) press RETURN to end the program. When you end the program you will have to press the SYSTEM RESET key to clear the screen.

Once you get used to drawing with the joystick you can create all kinds of different sketches and designs. The only limit is your imagination and patience.

```
10 REM *** JOYSTICK DRAWER ***
20 REM
30 DIM A$(1)
40 GRAPHICS 0
100 REM  *******
110 REM SET UP
120 REM  *******
130 PRINT CHR$(125)
140 PRINT ,"JOYSTICK DRAWER"
150 PRINT : PRINT "PLUG YOUR JOYSTICK INTO
JACK #1."
160 PRINT "PRESS RETURN WHEN YOU ARE
READY";
170 INPUT A$
180 PRINT : PRINT "INPUT X COORDINATE (0 -
318";
190 TRAP 180
200 INPUT X
210 IF X < 0 OR X > 318 THEN 180
220 PRINT : PRINT "INPUT Y COORDINATE (0 -
158)";
230 TRAP 220
240 INPUT Y
250 IF Y < 0 OR Y > 158 THEN 220
260 GRAPHICS 8
270 COLOR 3
280 PLOT X, Y
300 REM ********************
310 REM DRAWING ROUTINE
320 REM ********************
330 J = STICK(0)
340 I = STRIG(0)
350 IF I = 0 THEN GRAPHICS 0 : GOTO 180
360 KEY = PEEK(764)
370 POKE 764, 255
380 IF KEY = 33 THEN 630
390 IF KEY = 12 THEN PRINT "PROGRAM
ENDED." : END
```

```
400 IF X < 1 THEN X = 1
410 IF X > 318 THEN X = 318
420 IF Y < 1 THEN Y = 1
430 IF Y > 158 THEN Y = 158
440 POKE 755, 0
450 POKE 656, 0
460 PRINT "X = "; X; "      Y = "; Y; "    "
470 IF J = 15 THEN 330
480 IF J = 14 THEN Y = Y - 1 : GOTO 560
490 IF J = 6 THEN X = X + 1 : Y = Y - 1 :
GOTO 560
500 IF J = 7 THEN X = X + 1 : GOTO 560
510 IF J = 5 THEN X = X + 1 : Y = Y + 1 :
GOTO 560
520 IF J = 13 THEN Y = Y + 1 : GOTO 560
530 IF J = 9 THEN X = X - 1 : Y = Y + 1 :
GOTO 560
540 IF J = 11 THEN X = X - 1 : GOTO 560
550 IF J = 10 THEN X = X - 1 : Y = Y - 1
560 DRAWTO X, Y
570 GOTO 330
600 REM ****************
610 REM MOVE PLOTTER
620 REM ****************
630 J = STICK(0)
640 I = STRIG(0)
650 IF I = 0 THEN GRAPHICS 0 : GOTO 180
660 KEY = PEEK(764)
670 POKE 764, 255
680 IF KEY = 33 THEN PLOT X, Y : GOTO 330
690 IF KEY = 12 THEN PRINT "PROGRAM
ENDED." : END
700 IF X < 1 THEN X = 1
710 IF X > 318 THEN X = 318
720 IF Y < 1 THEN Y = 1
730 IF Y > 158 THEN Y = 158
740 POKE 656, 0
750 PRINT "X = "; X; "    Y = "; Y; "     "
```

```
760 IF J = 15 THEN 630
770 IF J = 14 THEN Y = Y - 1 : GOTO 630
780 IF J = 6 THEN X = X + 1 : Y = Y - 1 :
GOTO 630
790 IF J = 7 THEN X = X + 1 : GOTO 630
800 IF J = 5 THEN X = X + 1 : Y = Y + 1 :
GOTO 630
810 IF J = 13 THEN Y = Y + 1 : GOTO 630
820 IF J = 9 THEN X = X - 1 : Y = Y + 1 :
GOTO 630
830 IF J = 11 THEN X = X - 1 : GOTO 630
840 IF J = 10 THEN X = X - 1 : Y = Y - 1 :
GOTO 630
```

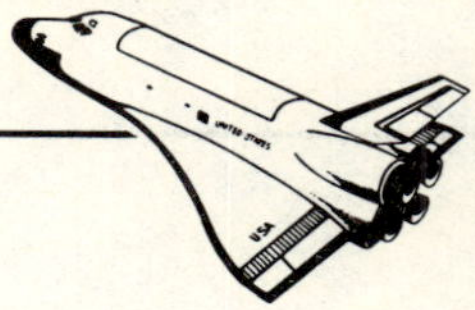

Craps

Here's one for all you high rollers or fantasy high rollers. This program is a craps game. You start the game with $100. Play continues until you lose all the money or decide to leave the 'table.' The program is a simple one in that it allows only 'PASS' and 'DON'T PASS' bets. Despite this, the game simulates the tenseness and fast action of craps rather well. As a programming exercise, you might want to expand the game to include COME, DON'T COME, ODDS, and PROPOSITION bets. Also, if you're the type to whom money is no object, you can change the value of M in line 40 so you can start the game with more than $100. It can be quite thrilling to wager $10,000 on a roll of the dice, even if it isn't the real thing. The program can be used as practice before your next trip to Las Vegas or Atlantic City.

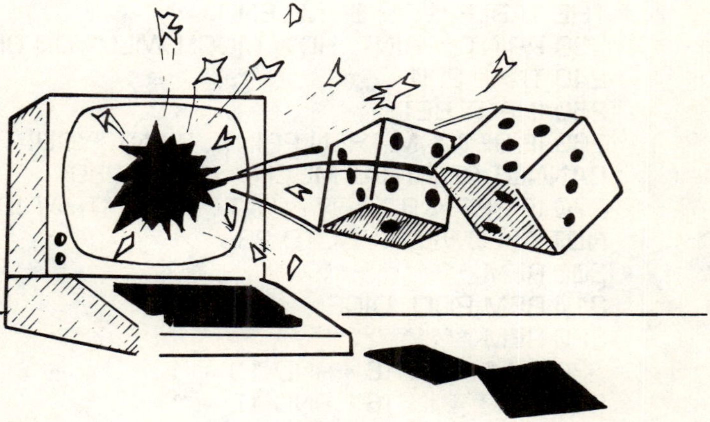

```
10 REM *** CRAPS GAME ***
20 REM
30 DIM A$(1)
40 M = 100
50 PRINT CHR$(125)
100 REM **************
110 REM PLACE A BET
120 REM **************
130 IF M = 0 THEN PRINT : PRINT “YOU ARE
OUT OF MONEY. GAME ENDED.” : END
140 PRINT : PRINT “YOU HAVE $”; M
150 PRINT : PRINT “HOW WILL YOU BET?”
160 PRINT : PRINT “1) PASS.”
170 PRINT “2) DON’T PASS.”
180 PRINT “3) LEAVE GAME.”
190 TRAP 160
200 INPUT B
210 IF B < 1 OR B > 3 THEN PRINT : PRINT
“ANSWER 1, 2, OR 3.” : GOTO 160
220 IF B = 3 THEN PRINT : PRINT “YOU LEAVE
THE TABLE WITH $”; M : END
230 PRINT : PRINT “HOW MUCH WILL YOU BET”;
240 TRAP 230
250 INPUT BET
260 IF BET > M THEN PRINT : PRINT “YOU
CANNOT BET THAT MUCH.” : GOTO 230
270 IF BET < 0 THEN PRINT : PRINT “THAT IS
NOT ALLOWED.” : GOTO 230
300 REM ************
310 REM ROLL DICE
320 REM ************
330 DIE1 = INT(6 * RND(1)) + 1
340 DIE2 = INT(6 * RND(1)) + 1
350 ROLL = DIE1 + DIE2
360 PRINT CHR$(125)
370 PRINT : PRINT “COMPUTER ROLLS A ”; ROLL
380 IF ROLL = 7 AND B = 1 THEN 490
390 IF ROLL = 7 AND B = 2 THEN 520
```

```
400 IF ROLL = 11 AND B = 1 THEN 490
410 IF ROLL = 11 AND B = 2 THEN 520
420 IF ROLL = 2 AND B = 1 THEN 520
430 IF ROLL = 2 AND B = 2 THEN 490
440 IF ROLL = 3 AND B = 1 THEN 520
450 IF ROLL = 3 AND B = 2 THEN 490
460 IF ROLL = 12 AND B = 1 THEN 520
470 IF ROLL = 12 AND B = 2 THEN 550
480 GOTO 570
490 PRINT : PRINT "YOU WIN!"
500 M = M + BET
510 GOTO 140
520 PRINT : PRINT "YOU LOSE."
530 M = M - BET
540 GOTO 130
550 PRINT : PRINT "PUSH. YOU KEEP YOUR BET."
560 GOTO 140
570 PNT = ROLL
580 PRINT : PRINT "WHEN YOU ARE READY FOR
NEXT ROLL,"
590 PRINT "PRESS THE RETURN KEY.";
600 INPUT A$
700 REM ************************
710 REM ROLL TO MAKE POINT
720 REM ************************
730 PRINT CHR$(125)
740 PRINT : PRINT "POINT TO MAKE IS   "; PNT
750 DIE1 = INT(6 * RND(1)) + 1
760 DIE2 = INT(6 * RND(1)) + 1
770 ROLL = DIE1 + DIE 2
780 PRINT : PRINT "COMPUTER ROLLS A ";ROLL
790 PRINT
800 IF ROLL = PNT AND B = 1 THEN 490
810 IF ROLL = 2 AND B = 2 THEN 490
820 IF ROLL = 2 AND B = 1 THEN 520
830 IF ROLL = PNT AND B = 2 THEN 520
840 IF ROLL = 7 AND B = 1 THEN 520
850 IF ROLL = 7 AND B = 2 THEN 490
860 GOTO 580
```

Role-Playing Game Dice Roller

Those of you who play role-playing games such as *Dungeons and Dragons* may find this program helpful. The game master in particular should profit from using this program. Those who regularly have to roll 20 dice "fireballs" and the like, will also appreciate the time and effort saved.

When RUN, the program will display a menu that lists the various types of dice that are used. You will notice the prompt 'What type?' directly under the menu. Simply enter the number for the type of die you want rolled. For example, you would enter '4' if you wanted a 10-sided die rolled. Next, you will be asked 'How many rolls?' Simply enter the number of times you want the die rolled. The third and final prompt will ask if you want the results of the die rolls added together. This is useful when you are rolling for weapon damage or rolling for a new character. After you answer the three prompts, the computer will display the results of each die roll. For a large amount of die rolls you will have to press the RETURN key to 'scroll' forward. The total of the rolls will be displayed at the end of the list. Happy gaming and 'may the dice be with you!'

```
10 REM *** ROLE - PLAYING DICE ROLLER ***
20 REM
30 DIM A$(1)
40 DIM ROLL(1000)
100 REM *************
110 REM USER INPUT
120 REM *************
130 PRINT CHR$(125)
140 FLAG = 0
150 PRINT : PRINT ,"DIE ROLLER"
160 PRINT : PRINT "1) 4 sided","2) 6 sided"
170 PRINT : PRINT "3) 8 sided","4) 10 sided"
180 PRINT : PRINT "5) 12 sided","6) 20 sided"
190 PRINT : PRINT "7) 100 'sided' (percentile)"
200 PRINT : PRINT "8) END PROGRAM"
210 PRINT : PRINT "What type";
220 TRAP 210
230 INPUT TYPE
240 IF TYPE < 1 OR TYPE > 8 THEN 210
250 IF TYPE = 8 THEN 820
260 PRINT : PRINT "How many rolls";
270 TRAP 260
280 INPUT NUM
290 IF NUM < 1 THEN 260
300 PRINT : PRINT "Add results (Y or N)";
310 INPUT A$
320 IF A$ = "Y" THEN FLAG = 1 : GOTO 400
330 IF A$ <> "N" THEN 300
400 REM ***********
410 REM ROLL DICE
420 REM ***********
430 ON TYPE GOTO 440, 450, 460, 470, 480,
490, 500
440 DIE = 4 : GOTO 510
450 DIE = 6 : GOTO 510
460 DIE = 8 : GOTO 510
470 DIE = 10 : GOTO 510
480 DIE = 12 : GOTO 510
```

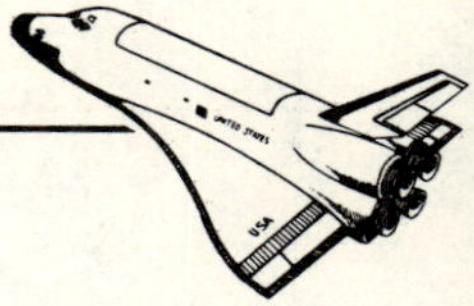

```
490 DIE = 20 : GOTO 510
500 DIE = 100
510 TOTAL = 0
520 FOR N = 1 TO NUM
530 ROLL(N) = INT(DIE * RND(1) + 1)
540 IF FLAG = 1 THEN TOTAL = TOTAL + ROLL(N)
550 NEXT N
600 REM *****************
610 REM PRINT RESULTS
620 REM *****************
630 PRINT CHR$(125)
640 PRINT : PRINT ,"RESULTS"
650 PRINT : PRINT "ROLL #","DIE ROLL"
660 PRINT
670 FOR N = 1 TO NUM
680 PRINT N, ROLL(N)
690 ROW = PEEK(84)
700 IF ROW >= 19 THEN 720
710 GOTO 770
720 PRINT : PRINT "PRESS RETURN TO CONTINUE";
730 INPUT A$
740 PRINT CHR$(125)
750 PRINT "ROLL #", "DIE ROLL"
760 PRINT
770 NEXT N
780 IF FLAG = 1 THEN PRINT : PRINT "TOTAL OF ROLLS = "; TOTAL
790 PRINT : PRINT "PRESS RETURN FOR MENU";
800 INPUT A$
810 GOTO 130
820 PRINT : PRINT "PROGRAM ENDED."
830 END
```

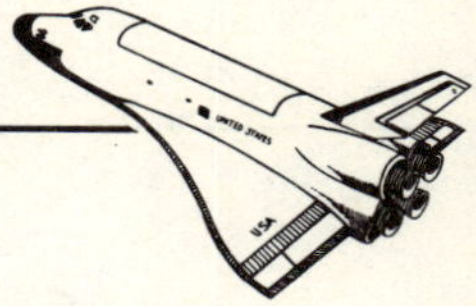

Role-Playing Character Generator

Here is a program for fantasy/sci-fi role playing gamers. With this program you can specify almost any set of characteristics you want your characters to have (no, you can't have 'ability to ward off a mugger while eating a hot dog and haggling with a merchant at 42nd and Eighth Avenue at 1:30 p.m.'). You can also specify the range of random numbers (i.e., die rolls) for each characteristic. The program will generate an almost limitless supply of characters 'rolled' to your specifications. You can display the characters on the screen and can also print them on your printer. The program also saves your specifications on a disk file named CHRSPEC.001 (lines 2030 - 2160).

You are now ready to create that Barbarian horde you've always dreamed about. Use them to conquer that kingdom of pesky elves to the north!

```
10 REM *** ROLE-PLAYING CHARACTER
GENERATOR ***
20 REM
30 DIM A$(1)
40 DIM DIE(100), SCORE(100)
50 PRINT CHR$(125)
60 PRINT : PRINT "Do you want instructions (Y or
N)";
70 INPUT A$
80 IF A$ = "N" THEN 890
90 IF A$ <> "Y" THEN 60
100 REM ****************
110 REM INSTRUCTIONS
120 REM ****************
130 PRINT CHR$(125)
140 PRINT ,"INSTRUCTION"
150 PRINT : PRINT " This program will generate
char-"
160 PRINT "acters for you to use with your role"
170 PRINT "playing games. It can be used for any"
180 PRINT "role playing system since you your-"
190 PRINT "self specify the characteristics and"
200 PRINT "number ranges used. Your specifica-"
210 PRINT "tions can be saved on disk or tape"
220 PRINT "for future use."
230 PRINT : PRINT "PRESS RETURN TO
CONTINUE";
240 INPUT A$
250 PRINT CHR$(125)
260 PRINT : PRINT " When you initially create your"
270 PRINT "specifications the computer will ask"
280 PRINT "you four questions:"
290 PRINT : PRINT " 1) What is the maximum
string"
300 PRINT " length of your characteristics?"
310 PRINT : PRINT " 2) How many characteristics
will"
320 PRINT " the characters have?"
```

```
330 PRINT : PRINT " 3) What are the names of the
diff-"
340 PRINT " erent characteristics?"
350 PRINT : PRINT " 4) What are the die roll
ranges"
360 PRINT " for each characteristic?"
370 PRINT : PRINT "PRESS RETURN TO
CONTINUE";
380 INPUT A$
390 PRINT CHR$(125)
400 PRINT : PRINT " What question 1 is asking is"
410 PRINT "to enter the length of the longest"
420 PRINT "characteristic name you are using."
430 PRINT "An example is the name
INTELLIGENCE."
440 PRINT "This word is 12 characters long. If"
450 PRINT "it were the longest name you were"
460 PRINT "using, your response to question 1"
470 PRINT "would be to type in '12' and press"
480 PRINT "the return key."
490 PRINT : PRINT "PRESS RETURN TO
CONTINUE";
500 INPUT A$
510 PRINT CHR$(125)
520 PRINT : PRINT " Question 2 is simply asking"
530 PRINT "how many characteristics each char-"
540 PRINT "acter will have. If you wanted each"
550 PRINT "character to consist of STRENGTH,
IN-"
560 PRINT "TELLIGENCE, and CONSTITUTION,
you"
570 PRINT "would respond by entering '3'."
580 PRINT : PRINT "PRESS RETURN TO
CONTINUE";
590 INPUT A$
600 PRINT CHR$(125)
610 PRINT : PRINT " Question 3 will actually be a "
620 PRINT "series of prompts that ask you to in-"
```

```
630 PRINT "put the names of each characteristic"
640 PRINT "used in creating your characters."
650 PRINT "Simply enter, one by one, the names"
660 PRINT "of each characteristic."
670 PRINT : PRINT "PRESS RETURN TO
CONTINUE";
680 INPUT A$
690 PRINT CHR$(125)
700 PRINT : PRINT " The final specifications you"
710 PRINT "will be asked to provide are the"
720 PRINT "number ranges for each character-"
730 PRINT "istic. Most role playing games use"
740 PRINT "a range of 3—18 (what this means is"
750 PRINT "that the sum of three six sided dice"
760 PRINT "are used to determine the character-"
770 PRINT "istic)."
780 PRINT : PRINT " You will be asked to provide"
790 PRINT "the low and high values for each"
800 PRINT "characteristic. Using the above ex-"
810 PRINT "ample, you would enter '3' for the"
820 PRINT "low value and '18' for the high val-"
830 PRINT "ue. The computer will ask you for"
840 PRINT "these values one at a time for each"
850 PRINT "characteristic."
860 PRINT : PRINT "YOU ARE NOW READY TO
BEGIN."
870 PRINT "PRES RETURN TO START";
880 INPUT A$
890 PRINT CHR$(125)
900 PRINT : PRINT "Do you wish to make new
specifi-"
910 PRINT "cations (Y or N)";
920 INPUT A$
930 IF A$ = "Y" THEN 1030
940 IF A$ = "N" THEN 2230
950 GOTO 890
1000 REM ******************************
1010 REM SPECIFY CHARACTERISTICS
```

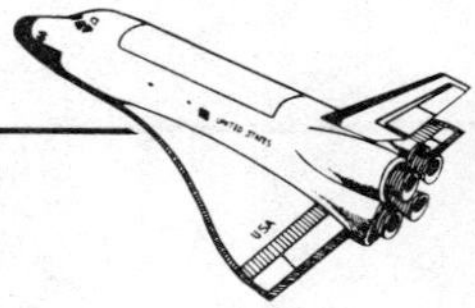

```
1020 REM ****************************
1030 PRINT CHR$(125)
1040 PRINT : PRINT "What is the string length of
the"
1050 PRINT "longest characteristic name";
1060 TRAP 1040
1070 INPUT LENGTH
1080 IF LENGTH < 1 OR LENGTH > 70 THEN
1040
1090 L = LENGTH - 1
1100 PRINT : PRINT "How many characteristics
will"
1110 PRINT "your characters have";
1120 TRAP 1100
1130 INPUT NUM
1140 IF NUM < 1 OR NUM > 50 THEN 1100
1150 DIM CONCAT$(LENGTH * NUM),
CAT$(LENGTH)
1160 DIM LOW(NUM), HIGH(NUM)
1170 FOR N = 1 TO LENGTH * NUM
1180 CONCAT$(N,N) = " "
1190 NEXT N
1200 PRINT CHR$(125)
1210 PRINT : PRINT "Input the name of each
character-"
1220 PRINT "istic."
1230 PRINT : PRINT "#","NAME"
1240 J = 1
1250 FOR N = 1 TO NUM
1260 PRINT N,
1270 INPUT CAT$
1280 IF LEN(CAT$) > LENGTH THEN 1260
1290 CONCAT$(J,J+L) = CAT$
1300 J = J + LENGTH
1310 NEXT N
1400 REM ***********************
1410 REM VERIFY INFORMATION
1420 REM ***********************
```

```
1430 PRINT CHR$(125)
1440 PRINT : PRINT "#", "NAME"
1450 PRINT
1460 J = 1
1470 FOR N = 1 TO NUM
1480 PRINT N, CONCAT$(J, J + L)
1490 J = J + LENGTH
1500 NEXT N
1510 PRINT : PRINT "Is the above information
correct (Y"
1520 PRINT "or N)";
1530 INPUT A$
1540 IF A$ = "Y" THEN 1630
1550 IF A$ <> "N" THEN 1510
1560 GOTO 1200
1600 REM *************************
1610 REM INPUT VALUE RANGES
1620 REM *************************
1630 PRINT CHR$(125)
1640 PRINT : PRINT "Input the low and high values"
1650 PRINT "for each characteristic."
1660 PRINT
1670 J = 1
1680 FOR N = 1 TO NUM
1690 PRINT CONCAT$(J, J + L), "LOW";
1700 TRAP 1690
1710 INPUT LOW
1720 PRINT CONCAT$(J, J + L), "HIGH";
1730 TRAP 1720
1740 INPUT HIGH
1750 LOW(N) = LOW
1760 HIGH(N) = HIGH
1770 J = J + LENGTH
1780 NEXT N
1800 REM *****************
1810 REM VERIFY RANGES
1820 REM *****************
1830 PRINT CHR$(125)
```

```
1840 J = 1
1850 FOR N = 1 TO NUM
1860 PRINT CONCAT$(J, J + L), LOW(N), HIGH(N)
1870 J = J + LENGTH
1880 NEXT N
1890 PRINT : PRINT "Is this information correct (Y or N)";
1900 INPUT A$
1910 IF A$ = "Y" THEN 1940
1920 IF A$ = "N" THEN 1630
1930 GOTO 1890
1940 PRINT : PRINT "Do you wish to store your specifi-"
1950 PRINT "cations on disk (Y or N)";
1960 INPUT A$
1970 IF A$ = "N" THEN 2530
1980 IF A$ <> "Y" THEN 1940
2000 REM ******************************
2010 REM CREATE SPECIFICATION FILE
2020 REM ******************************
2030 PRINT : PRINT "INSERT DATA DISK. PRESS RETURN";
2040 INPUT A$
2050 TRAP 2030
2060 OPEN #1, 8, 0, "D:CHRSPEC.001"
2070 PRINT #1; NUM
2080 PRINT #1; LENGTH
2090 J=1
2100 FOR N = 1 TO NUM
2110 PRINT #1; CONCAT$(J, J + L)
2120 PRINT #1; LOW(N)
2130 PRINT #1; HIGH(N)
2140 J = J + LENGTH
2150 NEXT N
2160 CLOSE #1
2170 GOTO 2530
```

```
2200 REM *****************************
2210 REM INPUT SPECIFICATION FILE
2220 REM *******************************
2230 PRINT : PRINT "INSERT DATA DISK. PRESS
RETURN";
2240 INPUT A$
2250 TRAP 2230
2260 OPEN #1, 4, 0, "D:CHRSPEC.001"
2270 INPUT #1; NUM
2280 DIM LOW(NUM), HIGH(NUM)
2290 INPUT #1; LENGTH
2300 L = LENGTH - 1
2310 DIM CONCAT$(NUM * LENGTH),
ELEM$(NUM * LENGTH)
2320 J = 1
2330 FOR N = 1 TO NUM
2340 INPUT #1; ELEM$
2350 CONCAT$(J, J + L) = ELEM$
2360 J = J + LENGTH
2370 INPUT #1; LOW
2380 LOW(N) = LOW
2390 INPUT #1; HIGH
2400 HIGH(N) = HIGH
2410 NEXT N
2420 CLOSE #1
2500 REM ****************************
2510 REM GENERATE CHARACTERS
2520 REM ****************************
2530 PRINT CHR$(125)
2540 PRINT : PRINT "How many characters do you
want";
2550 TRAP 2540
2560 INPUT AMOUNT
2570 IF AMOUNT < 1 THEN PRINT : PRINT
"PROGRAM ENDED." : END
2580 PRINT : PRINT " 1) VIEW CHARACTERS ON
SCREEN"
2590 PRINT : PRINT " 2) HARD COPY PRINT OF
CHARACTERS"
```

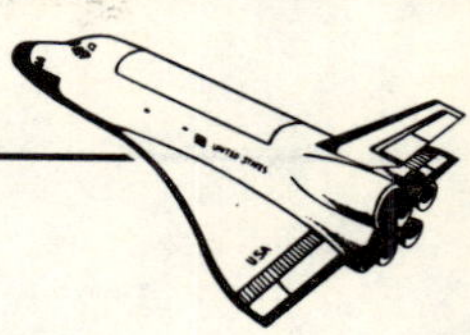

```
2600 PRINT : PRINT " 3) BOTH"
2610 PRINT : PRINT "What option do you want";
2620 TRAP 2610
2630 INPUT OPTION
2640 IF OPTION < 1 OR OPTION > 3 THEN 2610
2650 ON OPTION GOTO 2660, 2670, 2680
2660 FLAG = 1 : GOTO 2710
2670 FLAG = 2
2680 PRINT : PRINT "TURN ON PRINTER. ALIGN
PAPER."
2690 PRINT "PRESS RETURN TO CONTINUE";
2700 INPUT A$
2710 FOR N = 1 TO NUM
2720 DIE(N) = INT(HIGH(N) / LOW(N))
2730 NEXT N
2740 FOR N = 1 TO NUM
2750 SCORE(N) = 0
2760 FOR TIMES = 1 TO LOW(N)
2770 ROLL = INT(DIE(N) * RND(0)) + 1
2780 SCORE(N) = SCORE(N) + ROLL
2790 NEXT TIMES
2800 NEXT N
2810 COUNT = COUNT + 1
2900 REM *****************************
2910 REM PRINT OUT CHARACTERS
2920 REM *****************************
2930 IF FLAG = 1 THEN 3130
2940 J = 1
2950 LPRINT "CHARACTER #"; COUNT
2960 FOR N = 1 TO NUM
2970 LPRINT
2980 LPRINT CONCAT$(J, J + L), SCORE(N)
2990 LINES = LINES + 1
3000 J = J + LENGTH
3010 NEXT N
3020 FOR X = 1 TO 62 - (3 + LINES)
3030 LPRINT
3040 NEXT X
```

```
3050 IF COUNT = AMOUNT AND FLAG = 2
THEN 3250
3060 IF FLAG = 2 THEN 2710
3100 REM ******************
3120 REM SCREEN OUTPUT
3130 REM ******************
3130 J = 1
3140 PRINT CHR$(125)
3150 PRINT "CHARACTER #"; COUNT
3160 PRINT
3170 FOR N = 1 TO NUM
3180 PRINT CONCAT$(J, J + L), SCORE(N)
3190 J = J + LENGTH
3200 NEXT N
3210 IF COUNT = AMOUNT THEN 3250
3220 PRINT : PRINT "PRESS RETURN FOR NEXT
CHARACTER";
3230 INPUT A$
3240 GOTO 2710
3250 PRINT : PRINT "CHARACTERS GENERATED
PROGRAM ENDED."
3260 END
```

Section 4

Programs for Business

- Interest Calculator
- Profit Calculator
- Appointment Log
- Expense Log
- Auto Trip Log
- Inventory File

BUSINESS APPLICATIONS

The programs in this section focus on using your Atari to help you conduct your business activities. The main feature of most business programs is the creation and maintenance of data files. Of the programs in this section, the last four set up data files. The first two programs will make calculations but do not create files. The Interest and Profit programs will calculate interest earnings and sales profit. The next program is an Appointment log to keep track of appointments. The Expense log lets you organize your records without a lot of messy paperwork. Also included is a log to list your Auto Trips. Finally, there is a program for you to keep track of and update Inventory.

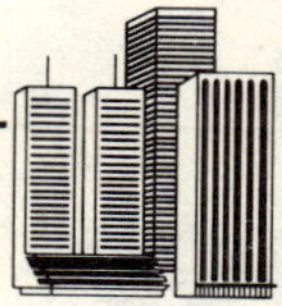

Interest Calculator

This program will calculate interest earnings. It can be used to figure interest payments on loans, bond dividends, and savings accounts. You only have to answer three questions: 1) what the principal amount is, 2) what the yearly interest rate is, and 3) the number of years you are allowing the interest to accumulate. If your principal has a maturity period of less than one year, you can still use the program. When the computer asks you how many 'years,' just respond by entering the number of maturity periods you are allowing the principal to mature.

```
10 REM *** INTEREST CALCULATOR ***
20 REM
30 DIM A$(1)
100 REM  *************
110 REM USER INPUT
120 REM  *************
130 T = 0
140 PRINT CHR$(125)
150 PRINT : PRINT "How much is the principal"
160 PRINT "(enter only a number)";
170 TRAP 150
180 INPUT P
190 T = P
200 PRINT : PRINT "What is the yearly interest
rate?"
210 PRINT "(enter a number only)";
220 TRAP 200
230 INPUT I
240 PRINT : PRINT "How many years are you
allowing the"
250 PRINT "account to mature";
260 TRAP 240
270 INPUT Y
300 REM *************************************
310 REM CALCULATE INTEREST EARNINGS
320 REM *************************************
330 PRINT CHR$(125)
340 PRINT : PRINT "YEAR","AMOUNT"
350 FOR L = 1 TO Y
360 T = T + INT (100 * (T * (1 + I / 100) - T) +
0.5) /100
370 PRINT L,"$";T
380 ROW = PEEK(84)
390 IF ROW >= 20 THEN PRINT : PRINT "PRESS
RETURN TO CONTINUE": INPUT A$
400 IF ROW >= 20 THEN PRINT CHR$(125)
410 NEXT L
420 PRINT : PRINT "Do you wish to run the program
again?"
```

```
430 PRINT "(Answer Y or N)";
440 TRAP 430
450 INPUT A$
460 IF A$ = "Y" THEN 130
470 IF A$ <> "N" THEN 430
480 PRINT CHR$(125)
490 PRINT : PRINT "Program ended."
500 END
```

Profit Calculator

This program can help figure out how much profit you make on sales of your products. The program also calculates how much a person receiving commission on sales will receive. The program will keep track of the accumulated profit from all sales of the product. This is handy because most businesses give different discounts for different sales. The program uses the following parameters to determine the profit:

1) The cost of producing a single unit (this includes the cost of labor).

2) The list price of the product.

3) The volume being sold.

4) The discount percentage offered the distributor.

5) The percentage given as commission.

When you RUN the program you will be asked to input the values for each of the above parameters. You can change the values for each particular sale. One change in the program you might want to make is to change the word 'inventor' to 'salesman.' The word appears in lines 1070 and 1120.

```
10 REM *** PROFIT AND COMMISSION
CALCULATOR ***
20 REM
30 DIM A$(1)
40 PRINT CHR$(125)
45 PRINT, "PROFIT CALCULATOR"
50 PRINT : PRINT "Do you want instructions (Y or
N)";
60 INPUT A$
70 IF A$ = "N" THEN 530
80 IF A$ <> "Y" THEN 50
100 REM ****************
110 REM INSTRUCTIONS
120 REM ****************
130 PRINT CHR$(125)
140 PRINT : PRINT, "INSTRUCTIONS"
150 PRINT : PRINT " This program will calculate
the"
160 PRINT "profit a manufacturer realizes on a "
170 PRINT "product. The computer will ask you to"
180 PRINT "input values for five different vari-"
190 PRINT "ables. The variables (and how to re-"
200 PRINT "spond to them) are: 1) Cost to pro-"
210 PRINT "duce (include labor) - input amount"
220 PRINT "(omit dollar sign) 2) List price -"
230 PRINT "input price (omit $) 3) Volume -"
240 PRINT "input number of units sold 4) Dis-"
250 PRINT "count - input discount percentage"
260 PRINT "given distributor 5) Commission -"
270 PRINT "input percentage of gross profit"
280 PRINT "given as commission. To input a"
290 PRINT "value, type the value and press"
```

```
300 PRINT "RETURN. Do not input commas or
dollar"
310 PRINT "signs."
320 PRINT : PRINT "PRESS THE RETURN KEY
WHEN READY FOR"
330 PRINT "REMAINDER";
340 INPUT A$
350 PRINT CHR$(125)
360 PRINT : PRINT " After you input the values for"
370 PRINT "these variables the computer will"
380 PRINT "calculate the net profit of the man-"
390 PRINT "ufacturer and the commission due the"
400 PRINT "inventor."
410 PRINT : PRINT " You are now ready to run the"
420 PRINT "program. Press the RETURN key when"
430 PRINT "you want to start."
440 INPUT A$
500 REM  *************
510 REM USER INPUT
520 REM  *************
530 TPROF1 = 0
540 TPROF2 = 0
550 PRINT CHR$(125)
560 PRINT : PRINT "WHAT IS THE PRODUCTION
COST PER UNIT"
570 PRINT "(INCLUDE LABOR COSTS)";
580 TRAP 570
590 INPUT COST
600 PRINT : PRINT "WHAT IS THE LIST PRICE OF
THE PRO-"
610 PRINT "DUCT";
620 TRAP 600
630 INPUT LIST
640 PRINT : PRINT "HOW MANY UNITS ARE
BEING SOLD";
650 TRAP 640
660 INPUT VOL
670 PRINT : PRINT "WHAT DISCOUNT
```

```
PERCENTAGE IS BEING"
680 PRINT "GIVEN THE DISTRIBUTOR";
690 TRAP 670
700 INPUT DIS
710 PRINT : PRINT "WHAT PERCENTAGE OF
PROFITS ARE BEING"
720 PRINT "GIVEN AS COMMISSIONS";
730 TRAP 710
740 INPUT COMM
800 REM *********************
810 REM CALCULATE PROFIT
820 REM *********************
830 REM
840 REM ** GROSS PROFIT **
850 GPROF = VOL * (((100 - DIS) / 100 * LIST)
- COST)
860 REM ** NET PROFIT **
870 NPROF = GPROF * (100 - COMM) / 100
880 TPROF1 = TPROF1 + NPROF
890 REM ** COMMISSION **
900 IPROF = GPROF * COMM / 100
910 TPROF2 = TPROF2 + IPROF
1000 REM **************
1010 REM PRINT PROFIT
1020 REM **************
1030 PRINT CHR$(125)
1040 PRINT : PRINT "Manufacturer's profit on sale"
1050 PRINT "is $";NPROF
1060 IF COMM = 0 THEN 1090
1070 PRINT : PRINT "Inventor's profit on sale"
1080 PRINT "is $";IPROF
1090 PRINT : PRINT "Manufacturer's total profit"
1100 PRINT "is $";TPROF1
1110 IF TPROF2 = 0 THEN 1140
1120 PRINT : PRINT "Inventor's total profit"
1130 PRINT "is $";TPROF2
1140 PRINT : PRINT "Do you wish to make another
sale"
```

```
1150 PRINT "(answer Y or N)";
1160 INPUT A$
1170 IF A$ = "Y" THEN PRINT CHR$(125):GOTO
640
1180 IF A$ <> "N" THEN 1140
1190 PRINT : PRINT "Do you wish to run the
program"
1200 PRINT "again (answer Y or N)";
1210 INPUT A$
1220 IF A$ = "Y" THEN 530
1230 IF A$ <> "N" THEN 1190
1240 PRINT : PRINT "PROGRAM ENDED."
1250 END
```

Appointment Log

Here is a program to help you keep track of your appointments. The program stores your appointments in a file named APPOINT.DAT. When you run the program you have the option to add, change, or delete appointments from the file. The program can also sort your appointments so they will appear in chronological order.

There are a few things you need to know about making entries in the log. When entering the date, use the format MMDD where MM is the month from 01 to 12 and DD is the day from 01 to 31. When you enter the time, use a 24 hour clock (0001–2400.) Your entries for date and time must be four characters long. This is so the appointments can be sorted properly. Also, your description of the appointment must not exceed 30 characters (this allows for clear viewing on a 40 column screen.) If you have an 80 column cartridge and you want to have more room for your descriptions, you can make the following changes:

```
30 DIM A$(6), DATE$(4), TIME$(4), APP$(70)
40 DIM ELEM$(78), FILE$(10000), REC$(70)
1100 IF LEN(APP$) > 70 THEN PRINT : PRINT
"TOO LONG" : GOTO 870
1900 FOR J = 1 TO COUNT * 78 : FILE$(J, J) = "
" : NEXT J
1990 FILE$(I + 8, I + 77) = APP$
2000 I = I + 78
2020 STRING = (COUNT - 1) * 78
2040 FOR P = 1 TO STRING - 77 STEP 78
2050 PL = P + 77
2060 PLEN = P + 78
2070 PLEN1 = P + 78
2180 APP$ = FILE$(I + 8, I + 77)
2190 I = I + 78
```

```
10 REM *** APPOINTMENT LOG ***
20 REM
30 DIM A$(6), B$(1), DATE$(4), TIME$(4),
APP$(30)
40 DIM ELEM$(38), FILE$(5000), REC$(30)
100 REM *************
110 REM USER INPUT
120 REM *************
130 PRINT CHR$(125)
140 PRINT ,"APPOINTMENT LOG"
150 PRINT : PRINT "INSERT DATA DISK."
160 PRINT : PRINT "PRESS RETURN WHEN
READY";
170 INPUT A$
180 CLOSE #1
190 CLOSE #2
200 TRAP 400
210 OPEN #1, 4, 0, "D:APPOINT.DAT"
220 OPEN #2, 8, 0, "D:APPOINT.TEM"
230 PRINT CHR$(125)
240 PRINT : PRINT " 1) ADD APPOINTMENT"
250 PRINT : PRINT " 2) UPDATE APPOINTMENT"
260 PRINT : PRINT " 3) REVIEW LOG"
```

```
270 PRINT : PRINT " 4) SORT LOG"
280 PRINT : PRINT " 5) LEAVE PROGRAM"
290 PRINT : PRINT "SELECT OPTION";
300 TRAP 290
310 INPUT OPTION
320 IF OPTION < 1 OR OPTION > 5 THEN 290
330 ON OPTION GOTO 700, 1200, 1500, 1810,
340
340 CLOSE #1
350 CLOSE #2
360 PRINT : PRINT "FILES CLOSED, PROGRAM
ENDED."
370 END
400 REM ******************
410 REM FILE NOT FOUND
420 REM ******************
430 PRINT CHR$(253)
440 PRINT : PRINT "FILE NOT FOUND ON THIS
DISK."
450 PRINT : PRINT "Either insert proper disk and
enter"
460 PRINT "'NEW' or enter 'CREATE' to create a"
470 PRINT "new file on this disk";
480 INPUT A$
490 IF A$ = "NEW" THEN 190
500 IF A$ <> "CREATE" THEN 450
600 REM *******************
610 REM CREATE NEW FILE
620 REM *******************
630 CLOSE #1
640 OPEN #1, 8, 0, "D:APPOINT.DAT"
650 PRINT #1; "END"
660 CLOSE #1
670 GOTO 180
700 REM ***********************
710 REM TRANSFER RECORDS
720 REM ***********************
730 COUNT = 0
```

```
740 INPUT #1; DATE$
750 IF DATE$ = "END" THEN 900
760 PRINT #2; DATE$
770 INPUT #1; TIME$
780 PRINT #2; TIME$
790 INPUT #1; APP$
800 PRINT #2; APP$
810 COUNT = COUNT + 1
820 GOTO 740
900 REM *********************
910 REM ADD APPOINTMENT
920 REM *********************
930 PRINT CHR$(125)
940 IF OPTION = 1 THEN PRINT "ADD
APPOINTMENT"
950 IF OPTION = 2 THEN PRINT "CHANGE
APPOINTMENT" : GOTO 970
960 PRINT : PRINT "ENTER 'END' WHEN DONE."
970 PRINT : PRINT "DATE. . ..";
980 INPUT DATE$
990 IF DATE$ = "END" THEN 2400
1000 IF LEN(DATE$) <> 4 THEN 970
1010 IF VAL(DATE$)< 101 THEN 970
1020 IF VAL(DATE$) > 1231 THEN 970
1030 PRINT : PRINT "TIME. . ..";
1040 INPUT TIME$
1050 IF LEN(TIME$) <> 4 THEN 1030
1060 IF VAL(TIME$) < 1 THEN 1030
1070 IF VAL(TIME$) > 2400 THEN 1030
1080 PRINT : PRINT "APPOINTMENT. . ..";
1090 INPUT APP$
1100 IF LEN(APP$) > 30 THEN PRINT : PRINT
"TOO LONG." : GOTO 1080
1110 PRINT : PRINT " 1) ADD"
1120 PRINT : PRINT " 2) CHANGE"
1130 PRINT : PRINT "SELECT OPTION";
1140 TRAP 1130
1150 INPUT OPT2
```

```
1160 IF OPT2 < 1 OR OPT2 > 2 THEN 1130
1170 IF OPT2 = 2 THEN 900
1180 IF OPTION = 1 THEN COUNT = COUNT + 1
1190 GOTO 2300
1200 REM ******************
1210 REM READ RECORDS
1220 REM ******************
1230 COUNT = 0
1240 INPUT #1; DATE$
1250 IF DATE$ = "END" THEN 2400
1260 INPUT #1; TIME$
1270 INPUT #1; APP$
1280 COUNT = COUNT + 1
1290 PRINT CHR$(125)
1300 PRINT : PRINT "DATE. . ..."; DATE$
1310 PRINT : PRINT "TIME. . ..."; TIME$
1320 PRINT : PRINT "APPOINTMENT. . ..."; APP$
1330 PRINT : PRINT " 1) KEEP"
1340 PRINT : PRINT " 2) CHANGE"
1350 PRINT : PRINT " 3) DELETE"
1360 PRINT : PRINT "SELECT OPTION";
1370 TRAP 1360
1380 INPUT OPT2
1390 IF OPT 2 < 1 OR OPT2 > 3 THEN 1360
1400 IF OPT2 = 3 THEN COUNT = COUNT - 1
1410 ON OPT2 GOTO 2300, 900, 1200
1500 REM ***************
1510 REM REVIEW LOG
1520 REM ***************
1530 PRINT CHR$(125)
1540 PRINT "Enter the date you want to review or"
1550 PRINT "enter ALL to review the entire log";
1560 INPUT A$
1570 IF A$ = "ALL" THEN 1600
1580 IF VAL(A$) < 101 THEN 1540
1590 IF VAL(A$) > 1231 THEN 1540
1600 PRINT CHR$(125)
1610 PRINT : PRINT "DATE      "; "TIME      ";
```

```
"APPOINTMENT"
1620 PRINT
1630 INPUT #1; DATE$
1640 IF DATE$ = "END" THEN 1730
1650 INPUT #1; TIME$
1660 INPUT #1; APP$
1670 IF A$ = "ALL" THEN PRINT DATE$; " ";
TIME$; " "; APP$
1680 IF A$ = DATE$ THEN PRINT DATE$; " ";
TIME$ " "; APP$
1690 ROW = PEEK(84)
1700 IF ROW = 20 THEN PRINT : PRINT "PRESS
RETURN TO CONTINUE"; : INPUT B$
1710 IF ROW = 20 THEN 1600
1720 GOTO 1630
1730 PRINT : PRINT "PRESS RETURN WHEN
FINISHED";
1740 INPUT A$
1750 GOTO 2400
1800 REM ***********
1810 REM SORT LOG
1820 REM ***********
1830 INPUT #1; REC$
1840 IF REC$ = "END" THEN 1860
1850 GOTO 1830
1860 INPUT #1; COUNT
1870 CLOSE #1
1880 IF COUNT < 2 THEN PRINT : PRINT "SORT
NOT REQUIRED." : GOTO 180
1890 PRINT : PRINT "STANDBY WHILE FILE IS
SORTED."
1900 FOR J = 1 TO COUNT * 38 : FILE$(J, J) = " "
: NEXT J
1910 I = 1
1920 OPEN #1, 4, 0, "D:APPOINT.DAT."
1930 INPUT #1; DATE$
1940 IF DATE$ = "END" THEN 2020
1950 FILE$(I, I + 3) = DATE$
```

```
1960 INPUT #1; TIME$
1970 FILE$(I + 4, I + 7) = TIME$
1980 INPUT #1; APP$
1990 FILE$(I + 8, I + 37) = APP$
2000 I = I + 38
2010 GOTO 1930
2020 STRING = (COUNT - 1) * 38
2030 FOR N = 1 TO COUNT - 1
2040 FOR P = 1 TO STRING - 37 STEP 38
2050 PL = P + 37
2060 PLEN = P + 38
2070 PLEN1 = P + 75
2080 IF FILE$(P, PL) <= FILE$(PLEN, PLEN1)
THEN 2120
2090 ELEM$ = FILE$(P, PL)
2100 FILE$(P, PL) =FILE$(PLEN, PLEN1)
2110 FILE$(PLEN, PLEN1) = ELEM$
2120 NEXT P
2130 NEXT N
2140 I = 1 : X = 1
2150 IF X > COUNT THEN 2400
2160 DATE$ = FILE$(I, I + 3)
2170 TIME$ = FILE$(I + 4, I + 7)
2180 APP$ = FILE$(I + 8, I + 37)
2190 I = I + 38
2200 X = X + 1
2300 REM **********************
2310 REM WRITE TO NEW FILE
2320 REM **********************
2330 PRINT #2; DATE$
2340 PRINT #2; TIME$
2350 PRINT #2; APP$
2360 ON OPTION GOTO 930, 1240, 1500, 2150,
340
2400 REM  **************
2410 REM CLOSE FILES
2420 REM  **************
2430 PRINT : PRINT "STANDBY WHILE FILES ARE
CLOSED."
```

```
2440 PRINT #2; "END"
2450 PRINT #2; COUNT
2460 CLOSE #1
2470 CLOSE #2
2480 IF OPTION = 3 THEN 2510
2490 XIO 33, #1, 0, 0, "D:APPOINT.DAT"
2500 XIO 32, #1, 0, 0, "D:APPOINT.TEM,
APPOINT.DAT"
2510 GOTO 210
```

Expense Log

Here is a program you can use to keep track of your expenses for the year. The program creates a file named TAX EXP. 'XXX' that stores the information. The 'XXX' is actually the last three digits of the year the file covers. This allows you to maintain a separate file for each year. The routine in lines 940 - 1150 creates new files. The program also gives you the option of printing out the file. This is useful in any number of situations. Lines 2630 - 2770 output the log to the printer. If you don't plan on using a printer you can delete lines 2500 - 2570 and 2600 - 2850. To shorten the boot-up time you can also delete the instructions.

```
10 REM *** EXPENSE ITEMS ***
20 REM
30 DIM A$(1), CAT$(3), DATE$(8), DES$(35)
40 DIM CAT1$(6), DATE1$(11), DES1$(38)
50 DIM COST1$(10), COST2$(10), COST3$(10),
PAD$(7)
60 DIM YEAR$(4), EXT$(3), FILE$(12)
70 FLAG = 0
80 PRINT CHR$(125)
90 PRINT ,"EXPENSE LOG"
100 PRINT : PRINT "Do you want the instructions?"
110 PRINT "Answer Y or N";
120 INPUT A$
130 IF A$ = "N" THEN 930
140 IF A$ <> "Y" THEN 110
200 REM ************************
210 REM USER INSTRUCTIONS
220 REM ************************
230 PRINT CHR$(125)
240 PRINT ,"INSTRUCTIONS"
250 PRINT : PRINT " When you run the program the
com-"
260 PRINT "puter will display, one at a time,"
270 PRINT "the following headings: 1)DATE 2)CAT."
280 PRINT "3)DESCRIPTION 4)EXPENSE."
290 PRINT : PRINT " You will notice that the
cursor"
300 PRINT "is located beside the DATE heading"
310 PRINT "and that a question mark (prompt) is"
320 PRINT "present. At this point, type in"
330 PRINT "the date the expense was incurred."
340 PRINT "The entry you make for the date"
350 PRINT "cannot exceed eight characters. After
you"
360 PRINT "type the date you must press the RE-"
370 PRINT "TURN key. At this point, you will no-"
380 PRINT "tice the prompt move to a position"
390 PRINT "beside the CAT. heading."
```

```
400 PRINT : PRINT "PRESS THE RETURN KEY
WHEN READY"
410 PRINT "FOR MORE INSTRUCTIONS";
420 INPUT A$
430 PRINT CHR$(125)
440 PRINT : PRINT " The CAT. heading is where you
en-"
450 PRINT "ter the type of expense incurred. En-"
460 PRINT "ter one of the following codes for"
470 PRINT "the CAT. heading:"
480 PRINT : PRINT " CODE",,"DEFINITION"
490 PRINT : PRINT " BUS",,"Business expense"
500 PRINT " EDU",,"Educational"
510 PRINT "INT",,"Interest payments
520 PRINT " MED",,"Uninsured medical"
530 PRINT " ",,"expenses"
540 PRINT : PRINT "You can use your own codes
for"
550 PRINT "the CAT. heading, as long as they do"
560 PRINT "not exceed 3 characters."
570 PRINT : PRINT "PRESS THE RETURN KEY
WHEN READY FOR"
580 PRINT "MORE INSTRUCTIONS";
590 INPUT A$
600 PRINT CHR$(125)
610 PRINT : PRINT " Next the cursor will be posit-"
620 PRINT "ioned beside the DESCRIPTION
heading."
630 PRINT "At this point, enter a brief de-"
640 PRINT "scription of the expense. For exam-"
650 PRINT "ple, you might enter 'MEDICATION'"
660 PRINT "or 'SCHOOL BOOKS.' The only limi-"
670 PRINT "tation is that each entry be no"
680 PRINT "more than 35 characters in length."
690 PRINT "Remember, to enter an item you type"
700 PRINT "it and then press the RETURN key."
710 PRINT : PRINT "PRESS THE RETURN KEY
WHEN READY"
```

```
720 PRINT "FOR MORE INSTRUCTIONS";
730 INPUT A$
740 PRINT CHR$(125)
750 PRINT : PRINT " The final heading you will make"
760 PRINT "an entry for is the EXPENSE heading."
770 PRINT "After you make your entry for the DE-"
780 PRINT "SCRIPTION heading the prompt will ap-"
790 PRINT "pear beside the EXPENSE heading. At"
800 PRINT "this point, type the amount of the"
810 PRINT "expense (do not type a dollar sign)"
820 PRINT "and press the RETURN key."
830 PRINT : PRINT " You are now ready to run the
pro-"
840 PRINT "gram. Be sure to check your entries"
850 PRINT "for accuracy before entering them."
860 PRINT : PRINT "PRESS THE RETURN KEY
WHEN YOU ARE"
870 PRINT "READY TO RUN THE PROGRAM";
880 INPUT A$
900 REM **************
910 REM USER INPUT
920 REM **************
930 PRINT CHR$(125)
940 PRINT : PRINT "Start a new file (Y or N)";
950 INPUT A$
960 IF A$ = "N" THEN 1030
970 IF A$ <> "Y" THEN 940
980 PRINT : PRINT "What year will the file cover";
990 TRAP 980
1000 INPUT Y
1010 X = 1
1020 GOTO 1070
1030 PRINT : PRINT "What year do you want to
access";
1040 TRAP 1030
1050 INPUT Y
1060 X = 2
1070 YEAR$ = STR$(Y)
```

```
1080 IF LEN(YEAR$) <> 4 THEN ON X GOTO
980, 1030
1090 EXT$ = YEAR$(2, 4)
1100 FILE$(1, 9) = "D:TAXEXP."
1110 FILE$(10, 12) = EXT$
1120 ON X GOTO 1130, 1170
1130 OPEN #1, 8, 0, FILE$
1140 PRINT #1, Y
1150 CLOSE #1
1160 GOTO 1230
1170 PRINT CHR$(253) : PRINT "INSERT DATA
DISK. PRESS RETURN";
1180 INPUT A$
1190 TRAP 1170
1200 OPEN #1, 4, 0, FILE$
1210 INPUT #1; Y
1220 CLOSE #1
1230 PRINT : PRINT "Do you wish to make an
entry"
1240 PRINT "(answer Y or N)"
1250 INPUT A$
1260 IF A$ = "N" THEN FLAG = 3 : GOTO 2040
1270 IF A$ <> "Y" THEN 1230
1280 PRINT CHR$(125)
1290 PRINT : PRINT "DATE........... ";
1300 INPUT DATE$
1310 PRINT: PRINT "CAT ...........";
1320 INPUT CAT$
1330 PRINT : PRINT "DESCRIPTION...... ";
1340 INPUT DES$
1350 PRINT : PRINT "EXPENSE...........";
1360 TRAP 1350
1370 INPUT E
1380 IF E < 0.01 THEN 1350
1400 REM ****************
1410 REM FORMAT DATA
1420 REM ****************
1430 FOR I = 1 TO 11
```

```
1440 DATE1$(I, I) = " "
1450 NEXT I
1460 DATE1$(1, 8) = DATE$
1470 FOR I = 1 TO 6
1480 CAT1$(I, I) = " "
1490 NEXT I
1500 CAT1$(1, 3) = CAT$
1510 FOR I = 1 TO 38
1520 DES1$(I, I) = " "
1530 NEXT I
1540 DES1$(1, 35) = DES$
1550 E = E + 1.0E - 03
1560 COST1$ = " "
1570 COST2$ = " "
1580 COST3$ = " "
1590 COST1$ = STR$(E)
1600 L = LEN(COST1$)
1610 COST2$(1, 1) = "$"
1620 COST2$(2, L) = COST1$(1, L - 1)
1630 L = LEN(COST2$)
1640 IF L = 10 THEN COST3$ = COST2$ : GOTO
1730
1650 FOR I = 1 TO 10 - L
1660 PAD$(I, I) = " "
1670 NEXT I
1680 COST3$(1, 10 - L) = PAD$
1690 COST3$(11 - L, 10) = COST2$
1700 REM ****************
1710 REM DISPLAY DATA
1720 REM ****************
1730 PRINT CHR$(125)
1740 PRINT "DATE .......... "; DATE1$
1750 PRINT "CATEGORY.......... "; CAT1$
1760 PRINT "DESCRIPTION...... "; DES1$
1770 PRINT "EXPENSE .............. "; COST3$
1780 PRINT
1790 COUNT = COUNT + 1
1800 IF COUNT = 3 THEN PRINT : PRINT "PRESS
```

```
RETURN TO CONTINUE"; : INPUT A$
1810 IF COUNT = 3 THEN COUNT = 0 : PRINT
CHR$(125)
1820 IF FLAG = 1 THEN RETURN
1830 PRINT : PRINT "Is the above data correct
(answer"
1840 PRINT "Y or N)";
1850 INPUT A$
1860 IF A$ = "N" THEN 1280
1870 IF A$ <> "Y" THEN 1830
1880 COUNT = 0
1900 REM **************
1910 REM APPEND FILE
1920 REM **************
1930 OPEN #1, 9, 0, FILE$
1940 PRINT #1; DATE1$
1950 PRINT #1; CAT1$
1960 PRINT #1; DES1$
1970 PRINT #1; COST3$
1980 CLOSE #1
1990 PRINT : PRINT "Do you wish to make another
entry"
2000 PRINT "(answer Y or N)";
2010 INPUT A$
2020 IF A$ = "Y" THEN 1280
2030 IF A$ <> "N" THEN 1990
2040 PRINT : PRINT "Do you wish to look at the
file"
2050 PRINT "(answer Y or N)";
2060 INPUT A$
2070 IF A$ = "Y" THEN 2230
2080 IF A$ <> "N" THEN 2040
2090 IF FLAG = 3 THEN 2530
2100 PRINT : PRINT "File has been appended,
program ended."
2110 END
2200 REM ***********
2210 REM INPUT FILE
```

```
2220 REM ***********
2230 FLAG = 1
2240 PRINT CHR$(125)
2250 OPEN #1, 4, 0, FILE$
2260 INPUT #1, Y
2270 TRAP 2380
2280 INPUT #1; DATE1$
2290 INPUT #1; CAT1$
2300 INPUT #1; DES1$
2310 INPUT #1; COST3$
2320 IF FLAG = 2 THEN RETURN
2330 GOSUB 1740
2340 GOTO 2270
2350 REM
2360 REM ** CHECK IF OUT OF DATA **
2370 REM
2380 ERROR = PEEK(195)
2390 IF ERROR <> 136 THEN PRINT : PRINT
"ERROR- "; ERROR : END
2400 CLOSE #1
2500 REM **************
2510 REM HARD COPY?
2520 REM **************
2530 PRINT : PRINT "Do you want a hard copy of
the data"
2540 PRINT "(answer Y or N)";
2550 INPUT A$
2560 IF A$ = "Y" THEN 2630
2570 IF A$ <> "N" THEN 2530
2580 PRINT : PRINT "PROGRAM ENDED"
2590 END
2600 REM *******************
2610 REM PRINT HARD COPY
2620 REM *******************
2630 FLAG = 2
2640 OPEN #1, 4, 0, FILE$
2650 INPUT #1; Y
2660 PRINT CHR$(125)
```

```
2670 PRINT : PRINT "TURN ON THE PRINTER,
ALIGN PAPER."
2680 PRINT "PRESS THE RETURN KEY WHEN
READY";
2690 INPUT A$
2700 LPRINT : LPRINT " TAX DEDUCTABLE
EXPENSES FOR "; Y
2710 LPRINT
2720 LPRINT "DATE   CAT.   DESCRIPTION
EXPENSE"
2730 LPRINT
2740 TRAP 2810
2750 GOSUB 2280
2760 LPRINT DATE1$; CAT1$; DES1$; COST3$
2770 GOTO 2750
2780 REM
2790 REM ** CHECK IF OUT OF DATA **
2800 REM
2810 ERROR = PEEK(195)
2820 IF ERROR <> 136 THEN PRINT : PRINT
"ERROR- "; ERROR : END
2830 CLOSE #1
2840 PRINT : PRINT "PROGRAM ENDED"
2850 END
```

Auto Trip Log

With this program you can use your Atari to keep a log of your automobile trips. This is helpful for a variety of purposes.

The program creates a disk data file named TRIP.001. It is on this file that the information from your trips are stored. If you prefer to use a cassette recorder instead of a disk drive, make the following line changes:

```
240 PRINT : PRINT "CUE TAPE."
280 OPEN #1, 8, 0, "C:TRIP.001"
282 FOR I = 1 TO 128
284 PUT #1, 0
286 NEXT I
932 FOR N = 1 TO 4
934 PRINT #1; CHR$(253); CHR$(125)
936 NEXT N
1040 PRINT : PRINT "CUE TAPE."
1080 OPEN #1, 4, 0, "C:TRIP.001"
1082 FOR I = 1 TO 128
1084 GET #1, D
1086 NEXT I
1110 DELETE  LINE
1165 IF START$ = CHR$(253) THEN 1260
```

To save your file on tape, you must print out dummy records at the beginning and the end of the file. Lines 282–286 outputs a dummy record at the beginning of the file. Lines 932–936 outputs a dummy record at the end of the file. This record is called a trailer record. Notice that the number of elements in the trailer record corresponds with the actual record. One way to expand this program is by adding a routine to output the file to your printer. The Expense Log in this book has such a routine you can use.

```
10 REM *** AUTO TRIP LOG ***
20 REM
30 DIM A$(6), START$(16), END$(16), TRIP$(50),
NAT$(50)
40 PRINT CHR$(125)
50 PRINT : PRINT ,"AUTO TRIP LOG"
60 PRINT : PRINT "Is this a new or existing log
(reply"
70 PRINT "NEW or EXIST)";
80 INPUT A$
90 IF A$ = "EXIST" THEN 300
```

```
100 IF A$ <> "NEW" THEN 60
200 REM ******************
210 REM CREATE NEW FILE
220 REM ******************
230 PRINT CHR$(125)
240 PRINT : PRINT "INSERT DATA DISK"
250 PRINT "PRESS RETURN WHEN READY";
260 INPUT A$
270 TRAP 240
280 OPEN #1, 8, 0, "D:TRIP.001"
290 GOTO 450
300 REM ****************************
310 REM OPEN FILE, MAKE ENTRY
320 REM ****************************
330 PRINT : PRINT "Do you want to make a new
entry or"
340 PRINT "just review the log (answer ENTRY or"
350 PRINT "REVIEW)";
360 INPUT A$
370 IF A$ = "REVIEW" THEN 1030
380 IF A$ <> "ENTRY" THEN 330
390 PRINT CHR$(125)
400 PRINT : PRINT "INSERT DATA DISK."
410 PRINT "PRESS RETURN WHEN READY";
420 INPUT A$
430 TRAP 400
440 OPEN #1, 9, 0, "D:TRIP.001"
450 PRINT CHR$(125)
460 PRINT : PRINT "INPUT STARTING
DATE. . . . . .";
470 INPUT START$
480 PRINT : PRINT "INPUT DATE TRIP
ENDED. . . .";
490 INPUT END$
500 PRINT : PRINT "INPUT DESTINATION........";
510 INPUT TRIP$
520 PRINT : PRINT "NATURE OF TRIP ........ ";
530 INPUT NAT$
```

```
540 PRINT : PRINT "INPUT MILES TRAVELED......";
550 TRAP 540
560 INPUT MILES
570 IF MILES < 0 THEN 540
600 REM ****************
610 REM CHECK ENTRY
620 REM ****************
630 PRINT CHR$(125)
640 PRINT : PRINT "STARTING DATE. . . . . .";
START$
650 PRINT : PRINT "ENDING DATE. . . . . ."; END$
660 PRINT : PRINT "DESTINATION. . . . . ."; TRIP$
670 PRINT : PRINT "NATURE OF TRIP. . ."; NAT$
680 PRINT : PRINT "TOTAL MILES. . . . . ."; MILES
690 PRINT : PRINT "Is the above information
correct"
700 PRINT "(Y or N)";
710 INPUT A$
720 IF A$ = "N" THEN 450
730 IF A$ <> "Y" THEN 690
800 REM ****************
810 REM WRITE TO FILE
820 REM ****************
830 PRINT #1; START$
840 PRINT #1; END$
850 PRINT #1; TRIP$
860 PRINT #1; NAT$
870 PRINT #1; MILES
880 PRINT CHR$(125)
890 PRINT : PRINT "Do you wish to make another
entry"
900 PRINT "(Y or N)";
910 INPUT A$
920 IF A$ = "Y" THEN 450
930 IF A$ <> "N" THEN 890
940 CLOSE #1
950 PRINT : PRINT "Do you want to review the log"
960 PRINT "(Y or N)";
```

```
970 INPUT A$
980 IF A$ = “N” THEN PRINT : PRINT “PROGRAM
ENDED” : END
990 IF A$ <> “Y” THEN 950
1000 REM **************
1010 REM REVIEW LOG
1020 REM **************
1030 PRINT CHR$(125)
1040 PRINT : PRINT “INSERT DATA DISK.”
1050 PRINT “PRESS RETURN WHEN READY”;
1060 INPUT A$
1070 TRAP 1040
1080 OPEN #1, 4, 0, “D:TRIP.001”
1090 PRINT CHR$(125)
1100 COUNT = 0
1110 TRAP 1260
1120 INPUT #1; START$
1130 INPUT #1; END$
1140 INPUT #1; TRIP$
1150 INPUT #1; NAT$
1160 INPUT #1; MILES
1170 PRINT “STARTING DATE......”; START$
1180 PRINT “ENDING DATE ......... ”; END$
1190 PRINT “DESTINATION......... ”; TRIP$
1200 PRINT “NATURE OF TRIP.....”; NAT$
1210 PRINT “TOTAL MILES ......... ”; MILES
1220 COUNT = COUNT + 1
1230 IF COUNT = 3 THEN PRINT : PRINT
“PRESS RETURN TO CONTINUE”;
1240 IF COUNT = 3 THEN INPUT A$ :
GOTO 1090
1250 GOTO 1110
1260 CLOSE #1
1270 PRINT : PRINT “END OF FILE,
PROGRAM ENDED”
1280 END
```

Inventory File

This program will help keep track of your inventory. The program creates a data file named INVEN.DAT which stores the information. Each record in the file consists of four fields: 1) the item number, 2) the item name/model #, 3) the items' list price, and 4) the number of items in stock. Be sure to use a four digit number for the item number field (item #1 is #0001).

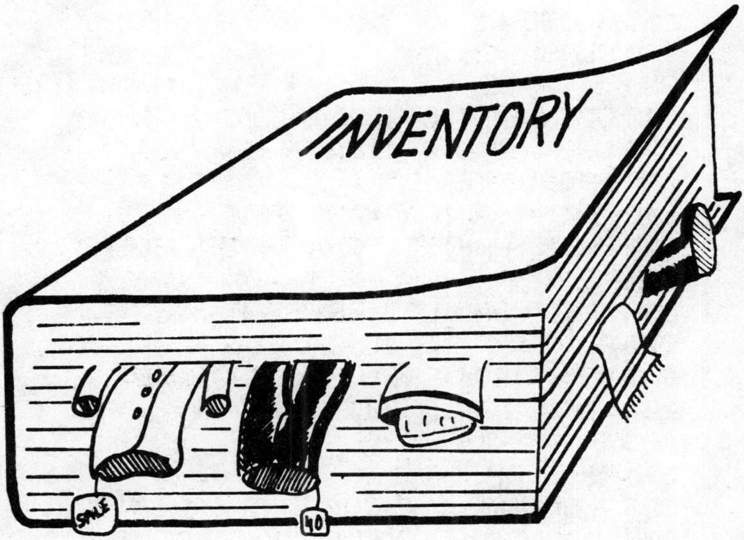

```
10 REM *** INVENTORY ***
20 REM
30 DIM A$(6), B$(4), ITNUM$(4), ITEM$(30),
LPRICE$(4), STOCK$(4)
40 DIM REC$(30), FILE(10000), ELEM$(45)
100 REM  *************
110 REM USER INPUT
120 REM  *************
130 PRINT CHR$(125)
140 PRINT ,"INVENTORY"
150 PRINT : PRINT "INSERT FILE DISK."
160 PRINT : PRINT "PRESS RETURN WHEN
READY";
170 INPUT A$
180 CLOSE #1
190 CLOSE #2
200 TRAP 400
210 OPEN #1, 4, 0, "D:INVEN.DAT"
220 OPEN #2, 8, 0, "D:INVEN.TEM"
230 PRINT CHR$(125)
240 PRINT : PRINT " 1) ADD ITEM"
250 PRINT : PRINT " 2) CHANGE OR DELETE
ITEM"
260 PRINT : PRINT " 3) REVIEW ITEM(S)"
270 PRINT : PRINT " 4) SORT LOG"
280 PRINT : PRINT " 5) LEAVE PROGRAM"
290 PRINT : PRINT "SELECT OPTION";
300 TRAP 290
310 INPUT OPTION
320 IF OPTION < 1 OR OPTION > 5 THEN 290
330 ON OPTION GOTO700,1300,1600,1900, 340
340 CLOSE #1
350 CLOSE #2
360 PRINT : PRINT "FILES CLOSED, PROGRAM
ENDED."
370 END
400 REM  *****************
410 REM FILE NOT FOUND
420 REM  *****************
```

```
430 PRINT CHR$(253)
440 PRINT : PRINT "FILE NOT FOUND ON THIS
DISK."
450 PRINT : PRINT "Either insert proper disk and
enter"
460 PRINT "'NEW' or enter 'CREATE' to create a"
470 PRINT "new file on this disk";
480 INPUT A$
490 IF A$ = "NEW" THEN 180
500 IF A$ <> "CREATE" THEN 450
600 REM *******************
610 REM CREATE NEW FILE
620 REM *******************
630 CLOSE #1
640 OPEN #1, 8, 0, "D:INVEN.DAT"
650 PRINT #1; "END"
660 CLOSE #1
670 POKE 195, 0
680 GOTO 180
700 REM ***********************
710 REM TRANSFER RECORDS
720 REM ***********************
730 COUNT = 0
740 INPUT #1; ITNUM$
750 IF ITNUM$ = "END" THEN 900
760 PRINT #2; ITNUM$
770 INPUT #1; ITEM$
780 PRINT #2; ITEM$
790 INPUT #1; LPRICE$
800 PRINT #2; LPRICE$
810 INPUT #1; STOCK$
820 PRINT #2; STOCK$
830 COUNT = COUNT + 1
840 GOTO 740
900 REM **********
910 REM ADD ITEM
920 REM **********
930 PRINT CHR$(125)
940 IF OPTION = 1 THEN PRINT "ADD ITEM"
```

```
950 IF OPTION = 2 THEN PRINT "CHANGE
ITEM":GOTO 970
960 PRINT : PRINT "ENTER 'END' WHEN DONE."
970 PRINT : PRINT "ITEM #......";
980 INPUT ITNUM$
990 IF ITNUM$ = "END" THEN 2500
1000 IF LEN(ITNUM$) <> 4 THEN 970
1010 IF VAL(ITNUM$) < 1 THEN 970
1020 PRINT : PRINT "ITEM.......";
1030 INPUT ITEM$
1040 IF LEN(ITEM$) > 30 THEN 1020
1050 PRINT : PRINT "LIST PRICE.......";
1060 TRAP 1050
1070 INPUT LPRICE
1080 LPRICE$ = STR$(LPRICE)
1090 IF VAL(LPRICE$) < 0.01 THEN 1050
1100 IF VAL(LPRICE$) > 9999.99 THEN 1050
1110 PRINT : PRINT "# IN STOCK.......";
1120 INPUT STOCK$
1130 IF VAL(STOCK$) < 0 THEN 1120
1140 IF VAL(STOCK$) > 9999 THEN 1120
1150 PRINT : PRINT " 1) ADD"
1160 PRINT : PRINT " 2) CHANGE"
1170 PRINT : PRINT "SELECT OPTION";
1180 TRAP 1170
1190 INPUT OPT2
1200 IF OPT2 < 1 OR OPT2 > 2 THEN 1180
1210 IF OPT2 = 2 THEN 900
1220 IF OPTION = 1 THEN COUNT = COUNT + 1
1230 GOTO 2400
1300 REM  ****************
1310 REM READ RECORDS
1320 REM  ****************
1330 COUNT = 0
1340 INPUT #1; ITNUM$
1350 IF ITNUM$ = "END" THEN 2500
1360 INPUT #1; ITEM$
1370 INPUT #1; LPRICE$
```

```
1380 INPUT #1; STOCK$
1390 COUNT = COUNT + 1
1400 PRINT CHR$(125)
1410 PRINT : PRINT "ITEM #......"; ITNUM$
1420 PRINT : PRINT "ITEM......"; ITEM$
1430 PRINT : PRINT "LIST PRICE......"; LPRICE$
1440 PRINT : PRINT "# IN STOCK......"; STOCK$
1450 PRINT : PRINT " 1) KEEP"
1460 PRINT : PRINT " 2) CHANGE"
1470 PRINT : PRINT " 3) DELETE"
1480 PRINT : PRINT "SELECT OPTION";
1490 TRAP 1480
1500 INPUT OPT2
1510 IF OPT 2 < 1 OR OPT2 > 3 THEN 1480
1520 IF OPT2 = 3 THEN COUNT = COUNT - 1
1530 ON OPT2 GOTO 2400, 900, 1340
1600 REM ****************
1610 REM REVIEW ITEMS
1620 REM ****************
1630 PRINT CHR$(125)
1640 PRINT : PRINT "Enter the item number you want to"
1650 PRINT "review or enter ALL to review the"
1660 PRINT "entire list";
1670 INPUT B$
1680 IF B$ = "ALL" THEN 1710
1690 IF VAL(B$) < 1 THEN 1640
1700 IF LEN(B$) > 4 THEN 1640
1710 PRINT CHR$(125)
1720 INPUT #1; ITNUM$
1730 IF ITNUM$ = "END" THEN NUM = 0 : GOTO 1880
1740 INPUT #1; ITEM$
1750 INPUT #1; LPRICE$
1760 INPUT #1; STOCK$
1770 IF B$ = "ALL" THEN 1790
1780 IF B$ <> ITNUM$ THEN 1720
1790 PRINT "ITEM #: "; ITNUM$
```

```
1800 PRINT "ITEM: "; ITEM$
1810 PRINT "LIST PRICE: $"; LPRICE$
1820 PRINT "# IN STOCK; "; STOCK$
1830 PRINT
1840 NUM = NUM+1
1850 IF NUM = 3 THEN PRINT : PRINT "PRESS
RETURN TO CONTINUE"; : INPUT A$
1860 IF NUM = 3 THEN NUM = 0 : PRINT
CHR$(125)
1870 GOTO 1270
1880 PRINT : PRINT "PRESS RETURN WHEN
FINISHED"; : INPUT A$
1890 GOTO 2400
1900 REM ************
1910 REM SORT LIST
1920 REM ************
1930 PRINT : PRINT "STANDBY WHILE FILE IS
SORTED."
1940 INPUT #1; REC$
1950 IF REC$ = "END" THEN 1970
1960 GOTO 1940
1970 INPUT #1; COUNT
1980 CLOSE #1
1990 IF COUNT = 0 THEN 2400
2000 IF COUNT = 1 THEN PRINT : PRINT "SORT
NOT REQUIRED." : GOTO 180
2010 FOR J = 1 TO COUNT * 45
2020 FILE$(J, J) = " "
2030 NEXT J
2040 I = 1
2050 OPEN #1, 4, 0, "D:INVEN.DAT"
2060 INPUT #1; ITNUM$
2070 IF ITNUM$ = "END" THEN 2170
2080 FILE$(I, I + 3) = ITNUM$
2090 INPUT #1; ITEM$
2100 FILE$(I + 4, I + 33) = ITEM$
2110 INPUT #1; LPRICE$
2120 FILE$(I + 34, I + 40) = LPRICE$
```

```
2130 INPUT #1; STOCK$
2140 FILE$(I + 41, I + 44) = STOCK$
2150 I = I + 45
2160 GOTO 2060
2170 STRING = (COUNT - 1) * 45
2180 FOR N = 1 TO COUNT - 1
2190 FOR P = 1 TO STRING - 44 STEP 45
2200 PL = P + 44
2210 PLEN = P + 45
2220 PLEN1 = P + 89
2230 IF FILE$(P, PL) <= FILE$(PLEN, PLEN1)
THEN 2270
2240 ELEM$ = FILE$(P, PL)
2250 FILE$(P, PL) = FILE$(PLEN, PLEN1)
2260 NEXT P
2270 NEXT N
2290 I = 1
2300 X = 1
2310 IF X > COUNT THEN 2500
2320 ITNUM$ = FILE$(I, I + 3)
2330 ITEM$ = FILE$(I + 4, I + 33)
2340 LPRICE$ = FILE$(I + 34, I + 40)
2350 STOCK$ = FILE$(I + 41, I + 44)
2360 I = I + 45
2370 X = X + 1
2400 REM **********************
2410 REM WRITE TO NEW FILE
2420 REM **********************
2430 PRINT #2; ITNUM$
2440 PRINT #2; ITEM$
2450 PRINT #2; LPRICE$
2460 PRINT #2; STOCK$
2470 ON OPTION GOTO 930, 1340, 180, 2310,
340
2500 REM  **************
2510 REM CLOSE FILES
2520 REM  **************
2530 PRINT : PRINT "STANDBY WHILE FILES ARE
CLOSED."
```

```
2540 PRINT #2; "END"
2550 PRINT #2; COUNT
2560 CLOSE #1
2570 CLOSE #2
2580 IF OPTION = 3 THEN 2610
2590 XIO 33, #1, 0, 0, "D:INVEN.DAT"
2600 XIO 32, #1, 0, 0,
"D:INVEN.TEM,INVEN.DAT"
2610 GOTO 180
```

Section 5

Utility Programs

- Printer Program Lister
- Dollar Formatter
- Printer Font Selector
- Binary-Hex-Decimal Converter
- List Sorter
- Julian Date Converter

UTILITY PROGRAMS

The final part of this book is devoted to utility programs. A utility is a program that helps you program or perform a procedure. Some utility programs help in using hardware such as printers or disk drives. Others are strictly software oriented. A good utility program is one that saves time performing a task or performs an otherwise impossible task. There are six utility programs in this section. The Program Lister and Number Converter can be classified as program development aids. The Dollar Formatter and Sort programs are useful as subroutines in your programs, although the Sort program works fine by itself. The Printer Font Selector is a program you can use when working with your printer. Finally, the Julian Date Converter can be used as a subroutine in programs where you are working with dates.

Program Listing Utility

The following short utility is quite helpful for editing and rewriting programs. Just add the program in the final lines of the program you are working on. When your program is finished RUNning, you will notice the prompt '?'. Simply press the RETURN key and the display screen will revert back to graphics mode 0 and your program will be listed. This is especially useful when you are testing a program that uses different graphic modes.

```
3000 REM *** PROGRAM LISTING UTILITY ***
3010 REM
3020 DIM AN$(1)
3030 INPUT AN$
3040 GRAPHICS 0
3050 LIST
```

Dollar Formatter

If you have been programming with your Atari you may have noticed what happens to numbers such as 5.00. If you haven't, what happens is the computer will print out the number "5.00" as "5". This can be irritating when you are working with dollar amounts, especially if you prefer 5.00 to 5. Another problem when working with dollar figures is right margin justification. That is lining up the numbers so all the decimal points are aligned. With this short subroutine you can take care of both problems.

Just before your program prints out a dollar amount insert the following statement: GOSUB 5000. The subroutine will format your variable so it has two decimal places with the right margin justified. What the routine does is convert your numeric variable to the string variable MONEY3$. The string MONEY3$ is 10 characters long. At the point in your program where you print your numeric variable print out the string variable MONEY3$ instead. If you deal with amounts above seven figures, you will have to change the DIMensions in line 30 and ther values 10 and 11 in lines 5090, 5100, 5130, and 5140. also, the best place for the DIM statement in line 50 is whereever you normally dimension your variables (to avoid an ERROR- 9). If you prefer, you can place the routine directly into your program rather than refer to it as a subroutine. Finally, you can add the following lines to test the program:

```
40 PRINT : PRINT "ENTER AMOUNT";
50 INPUT AMOUNT
60 GOSUB 5000
70 PRINT : PRINT MONEY3$
80 GOTO 40
```

Make sure the numeric variable in your program is identical to the one in lines 5030–5040.

```
10 REM *** DOLLAR FORMATTER ***
20 REM
30 DIM MONEY1$(10), MONEY2$(10),
MONEY3$(10), PAD$(7)
5000 MONEY1$ = " "
5010 MONEY2$ = " "
5020 MONEY3$ = " "
5030 AMOUNT = AMOUNT + .001
5040 MONEY1$ = STR$(AMOUNT)
5050 L = LEN(MONEY1$)
5060 MONEY2$(1,1) = "$"
5070 MONEY2$(2,L) = MONEY1$(1, L - 1)
5080 L = LEN(MONEY2$)
```

```
5090 IF L = 10 THEN MONEY3$ = MONEY2$ :
RETURN
5100 FOR I = 1 TO 10 - L
5110 PAD$(I, I) = " "
5120 NEXT I
5130 MONEY3$(1, 10 - L) = PAD$
5140 MONEY3$(11 - L, 10) = MONEY2$
5150 RETURN
```

Printer Font Selector

Use this program to change the font setting on your printer. The program was designed for a PROWRITER, but it may work on your printer (you'll have to check the printer manual). If it doesn't work for your printer, you can probably modify it so it will.

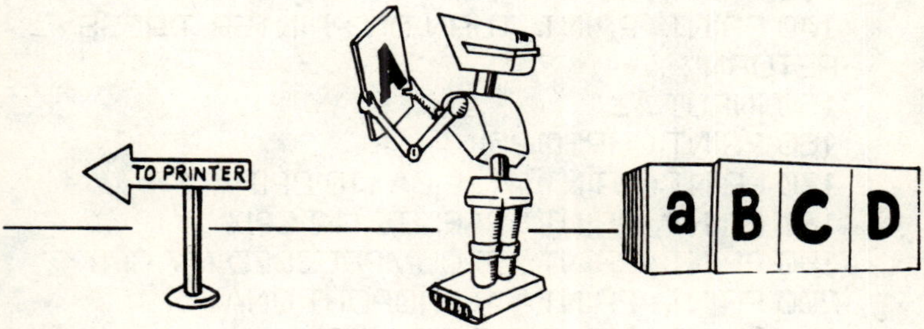

What the program does is redefine two character strings. PITCH$ sets the character pitch for the printer. TEXT$ sets the text type. When you choose an item from the menu, the program redefines the appropriate element of the string. When you have selected the font you want, the program routes the two strings to the printer (lines 1730, 1740) using the LPRINT statement. At that point you have the option to print a test line. If you experiment with different combinations of pitch and text, you will see that quite a few different fonts are possible.

```
10 REM *** PRINTER FONT SELECTOR ***
20 REM
30 PRINT CHR$(125)
40 DIM A$(1), PITCH$(2), TEXT$(5)
50 REM
60 REM ** CLEAR FONT STRINGS **
70 REM
80 PITCH$ = "  " : REM * 2 SPACES *
90 TEXT$ = "     " : REM * 5 SPACES *
100 REM ******************************
110 REM CHOOSE CHARACTER PITCH
120 REM ******************************
130 PRINT : PRINT ,"FONT SELECTOR"
140 PRINT : PRINT "TURN ON PRINTER. PRESS
RETURN";
150 INPUT A$
160 PRINT CHR$(125)
170 PRINT : PRINT " 1) PICA (10 CPI)"
180 PRINT : PRINT " 2) ELITE (12 CPI)"
190 PRINT : PRINT " 3) COMPRESSED (17 CPI)"
200 PRINT : PRINT " 4) PROPORTIONAL"
210 PRINT : PRINT "SELECT PITCH";
220 INPUT PITCH
230 IF PITCH < 1 OR PITCH > 4 THEN 150
240 PITCH$(1,1) = CHR$(27)
250 ON PITCH GOTO 300, 400, 500, 600
300 REM
310 REM ** PICA PITCH **
320 REM
330 PITCH$(2,2) = CHR$(78)
340 GOTO 700
400 REM
410 REM ** ELITE PITCH **
420 REM
430 PITCH$(2,2) = CHR(69)
440 GOTO 700
500 REM
510 REM ** COMPRESSED PITCH **
```

```
520 REM
530 PITCH$(2,2) = CHR(81)
540 GOTO 700
600 REM
610 REM ** PROPORTIONAL SPACE **
620 REM
630 PITCH$(2,2) = CHR$(80)
700 REM  *************************
710 REM CHOOSE SPECIAL TEXT
720 REM  *************************
730 PRINT CHR$(125)
740 PRINT : PRINT " 1) STANDARD"
750 PRINT : PRINT " 2) BOLDFACE TYPE"
760 PRINT : PRINT " 3) ELONGATED TYPE"
770 PRINT : PRINT " 4) UNDERLINED TYPE"
780 PRINT : PRINT " 5) BOLDFACE/ELONGATED"
790 PRINT : PRINT " 6) BOLDFACE/UNDERLINED"
800 PRINT : PRINT " 7) ELONGATED/
UNDERLINED"
810 PRINT : PRINT " 8) BOLDFACE/ELONGATED/
UNDERLINED"
830 PRINT : PRINT "SELECT TEXT";
840 TRAP 830
850 INPUT TEXT
860 IF TEXT < 1 OR TEXT > 8 THEN 830
870 TEXT$(1,1) = CHR$(27)
880 TEXT$(2,2) = CHR$(34)
890 TEXT$(3,3) = CHR$(27)
900 TEXT$(4,4) = CHR$(89)
910 TEXT$(5,5) = CHR$(15)
920 ON TEXT GOTO 1700, 1000, 1100, 1200,
1300, 1400, 1500, 1600
1000 REM
1010 REM ** BOLDFACE **
1020 REM
1030 TEXT$(2,2) = CHR$(33)
1040 GOTO 1700
1100 REM
```

```
1110 REM ** ELONGATED **
1120 REM
1130 TEXT$(5,5) = CHR$(14)
1140 GOTO 1700
1200 REM
1210 REM ** UNDERLINED **
1220 REM
1230 TEXT$(4,4) = CHR$(88)
1240 GOTO 1700
1300 REM
1310 REM ** BOLDFACE/ELONGATED **
1320 REM
1330 TEXT$(2,2) = CHR$(33)
1340 TEXT$(5,5) = CHR$(14)
1350 GOTO 1700
1400 REM
1410 REM ** BOLDFACE/UNDERLINED **
1420 REM
1430 TEXT$(2,2) = CHR$(33)
1440 TEXT$(4,4) = CHR$(88)
1450 GOTO 1700
1500 REM
1510 REM ** ELONGATED/UNDERLINED **
1520 REM
1530 TEXT$(4,4) = CHR$(88)
1540 TEXT$(5,5) = CHR$(14)
1550 GOTO 1700
1600 REM
1610 REM ** BOLDFACE/ELONGATED/
UNDERLINED **
1620 REM
1630 TEXT$(2,2) = CHR$(33)
1640 TEXT$(4,4) = CHR$(88)
1650 TEXT$(5,5) = CHR$(14)
1700 REM ***********
1710 REM SET FONT
1720 REM ***********
1730 LPRINT PITCH$
```

```
1740 LPRINT TEXT$
1750 PRINT CHR$(125)
1760 PRINT : PRINT "Do you want to print a test line"
1770 PRINT "(Y or N)";
1780 INPUT A$
1790 IF A$ = "Y" THEN 1900
1800 IF A$ <> "N" THEN 1760
1810 PRINT : PRINT "FONT IS SET. PROGRAM ENDED."
1820 END
1900 REM ***********
1910 REM TEST LINE
1920 REM ***********
1930 LPRINT "THIS IS WHAT THE FONT YOU HAVE CHOSEN LOOKS LIKE."
1940 GOTO 1810
```

Binary-Decimal-Hexadecimal Converter

This program converts binary, decimal, and hexadecimal numbers. When you input one type of number, the program calculates and displays the numbers equivalent in the other two number systems. Converting from binary to decimal is necessary when working with Atari player/missile graphics.

Hexadecimal numbers are used extensively in machine language. You'll find this program helpful until you become comfortable with the different number systems. Even then, the program is useful when converting large numbers.

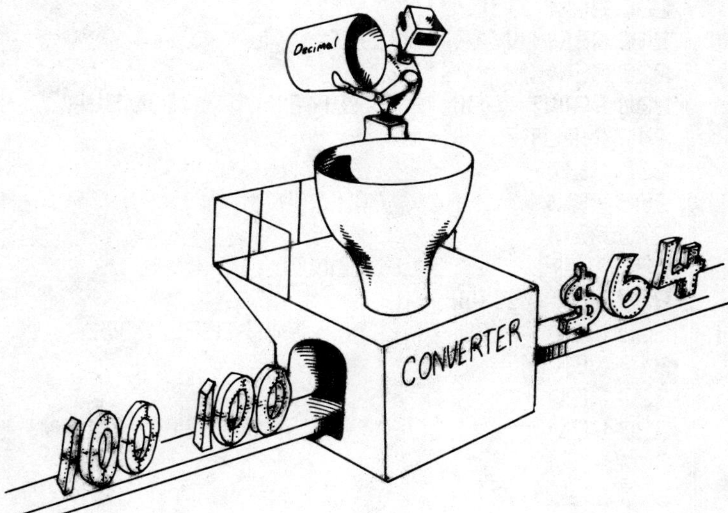

```
10 REM *** NUMBER CONVERTER ***
20 REM
30 DIM A$(1), BIN$(40), BINR$(40), HEX$(9),
HEXA$(1)
40 PRINT CHR$(125)
50 PRINT : PRINT " 1) DECIMAL TO HEX., BIN."
60 PRINT : PRINT " 2) BINARY TO DEC., HEX."
70 PRINT : PRINT " 3) HEXADECIMAL TO BIN.,
DEC."
80 PRINT : PRINT " 4) END PROGRAM."
90 PRINT : PRINT "SELECT OPTION";
100 TRAP 90
110 INPUT OPTION
120 IF OPTION < 1 OR OPTION > 4 THEN 90
130 PRINT CHR$(125)
140 ON OPTION GOTO 500, 200, 1000, 150
150 PRINT : PRINT "PROGRAM ENDED"
160 END
200 REM  **********************
210 REM BINARY TO DECIMAL
220 REM  **********************
230 PRINT : PRINT "ENTER BINARY NUMBER";
240 INPUT BIN$
250 REM
260 REM ** CHECK VALIDITY **
270 REM
280 FOR I = 1 TO LEN(BIN$)
290 N = ASC(BIN$(I,I))
300 IF N <> 48  AND  N <> 49 THEN 230
310 NEXT I
320 REM
330 REM ** CALCULATE DECIMAL EQUIVALENT **
340 REM
350 DEC = 0
360 POW = LEN(BIN$) - 1
370 FOR I = 1 TO LEN(BIN$)
380 IF VAL(BIN$(I,I)) = 1 THEN DEC = DEC +
2^POW
```

```
390 POW = POW - 1
400 NEXT I
410 DEC = INT(DEC + 0.1)
420 PRINT : PRINT "DECIMAL = "; DEC
500 REM ******************************
520 REM DECIMAL TO HEXADECIMAL
520 REM ******************************
530 IF OPTION <> 1 THEN 570
540 PRINT : PRINT "ENTER DECIMAL NUMBER";
550 TRAP 540
560 INPUT DEC
570 FOR I = I TO 9
580 HEX$(I,I) = " "
590 NEXT I
600 I = 9
610 DEC1 = DEC
620 DEC1 = DEC1
630 NUM = DEC1
640 DEC1 = INT(DEC1 / 16)
650 NUM = NUM - DEC1 * 16
660 IF NUM < 10 THEN HEX$(I,I) = STR$(NUM) :
GOTO 680
670 HEX$(I,I) = CHR$(NUM - 10 + 65)
680 IF DEC1 <> 0 THEN I = I - 1 : GOTO 620
690 PRINT : PRINT "HEX = "; HEX$(I,9)
700 IF OPTION = 1 THEN 800
710 PRINT : PRINT "PRESS RETURN WHEN
DONE";
720 INPUT A$
730 GOTO 40
800 REM *********************
810 REM DECIMAL TO BINARY
820 REM *********************
830 FOR I = 1 TO 40
840 BINR$(I,I) = " "
850 NEXT I
860 I = 40
870 DEC1 = DEC
```

```
880 DEC1 = DEC1
890 NUM = DEC1
900 DEC1 = INT(DEC1 / 2)
910 NUM = NUM - DEC1 * 2
920 BINR$(I,I) = CHR$(NUM + 48)
930 IF DEC1 <> 0 THEN I = I - 1 : GOTO 880
940 PRINT : PRINT "BIN = "; BINR$(I,40)
950 PRINT : PRINT "PRESS RETURN WHEN
DONE";
960 INPUT A$
970 GOTO 40
1000 REM ********************************
1010 REM HEXADECIMAL TO DECIMAL
1020 REM ********************************
1030 PRINT : PRINT "ENTER
HEXADECIMAL NUMBER";
1040 INPUT HEX$
1050 DEC = 0
1060 FOR I = 1 TO LEN(HEX$)
1070 HEXA$ = HEX$(I,I)
1080 IF HEXA$ < "0" THEN 1030
1090 IF HEX$(I,I) <= "9" THEN DEC =
DEC * 16 + VAL(HEXA$) : GOTO 1130
1100 IF HEXA$ > "F" THEN 1030
1110 IF HEXA$ < "A" THEN 1030
1120 DEC = DEC * 16 + ASC(HEXA$)
- ASC("A") + 10
1130 NEXT I
1140 PRINT : PRINT "DECIMAL = ";
DEC
1150 GOTO 800
```

List Sort

Sort programs are always handy. This program will sort records up to 99 characters (bytes) long. It is a simple sort in that the entire record is sorted as if it were one field. In other words, you cannot specify a field in the middle of a record to be the sort key. The key lines in the program are lines 490 and 630 - 780.

Line 490 takes each record you enter and concatenates them into one long string (CONCAT$). Lines 630 - 780 is where the sort actually happens. Each record in the file is compared to each subsequent record (line 730). If a record should appear after its subsequent record, then the two records swap positions in the string (lines 740 - 760). A good way to visualize what is happening is to think of the sort as a square dance where each record changes partners until all the records are in alphabetical order. Lines 860 - 950 split the sorted string and print out each record in its proper order.

```
10 REM *** LIST SORTER ***
20 REM
30 DIM A$(1)
100 REM *************
110 REM USER INPUT
120 REM *************
130 PRINT CHR$(125)
140 PRINT ,"LIST SORTER"
150 PRINT : PRINT "ENTER MAX. ITEM LENGTH";
170 INPUT LENGTH
180 IF LENGTH < 1 THEN 150
190 IF LENGTH > 99 THEN 150
200 PRINT : PRINT "ENTER NUMBER OF ITEMS";
220 INPUT NUM
230 IF NUM < 2 THEN PRINT : PRINT "IT
DOESN'T NEED TO BE SORTED." : GOTO 960
240 L = LENGTH - 1
250 DIM CONCAT$(LENGTH * NUM),
ELEM$(LENGTH)
300 REM ***************
310 REM CLEAR STRING
320 REM ***************
330 FOR N = 1 TO LENGTH * NUM
340 CONCAT$(N,N) = " "
350 NEXT N
400 REM ***************************
410 REM CONCATENATE STRINGS
420 REM ***************************
430 PRINT : PRINT "INPUT ITEMS TO BE SORTED"
440 PRINT
450 J = 1
460 FOR N = 1 TO NUM
470 PRINT "#"; N; " ";
480 INPUT ELEM$
490 CONCAT$(J,J+L) = ELEM$
500 J = J + LENGTH
510 NEXT N
520 PRINT : PRINT "PRESS RETURN TO SORT
```

```
ITEMS";
530 INPUT A$
540 PRINT : PRINT "STANDBY WHILE ITEMS ARE
SORTED."
600 REM *************
610 REM SORT ITEMS
620 REM *************
630 STRING = (NUM - 1) * LENGTH
640 FOR N = 1 TO NUM - 1
650 FOR P = 1 TO STRING - L STEP LENGTH
660 PL = P + L
670 PLN = P + LENGTH
680 PLN1 = P + LENGTH+L
690 REM
700 REM ** Compare adjacent substrings. If a
substring is less (in value)
710 REM than the subsequent substring, then swap
positions. **
720 REM
730 IF CONCAT$(P,PL) <= CONCAT$(PLN,PLN1)
THEN 770
740 ELEM$ = CONCAT$(P,PL)
750 CONCAT$(P,PL) = CONCAT$(PLN,PLN1)
760 CONCAT$(PLN,PLN1) = ELEM$
770 NEXT P
780 NEXT N
800 REM ***************
810 REM PRINT ITEMS
820 REM ***************
830 PRINT CHR$(125)
840 PRINT : PRINT ,"SORTED LIST"
850 PRINT : PRINT "ITEM #", "ITEM"
860 J = 1
870 FOR N = 1 TO NUM
880 PRINT N, CONCAT$(J,J + L)
890 J = J + LENGTH
900 ROW = PEEK(84)
910 IF ROW >= 20 AND N <> NUM THEN FLAG
= 1
```

```
920 IF FLAG = 1 THEN PRINT : PRINT "PRESS
RETURN TO CONTINUE";
930 IF FLAG = 1 THEN INPUT A$ : PRINT
CHR$(125)
940 IF FLAG = 1 THEN PRINT "ITEM #", "ITEM" :
FLAG = 0
950 NEXT N
960 PRINT : PRINT "PROGRAM ENDED."
970 END
```

Julian Date Converter

This program will convert a date in standard format to Julian format. For those who are not aware, the Julian calendar organizes the year into 365 days (366 for leap years). The Julian date for January 10, 1983 is 83.010. Julian dates are frequently used in data processing because of clarity and because it simplifies certain processes. It's easier to calculate a span of time by subtracting one Julian date from another, than it is to add the days of each month together. Note that the program will add an extra day for leap years (lines 530 - 570).

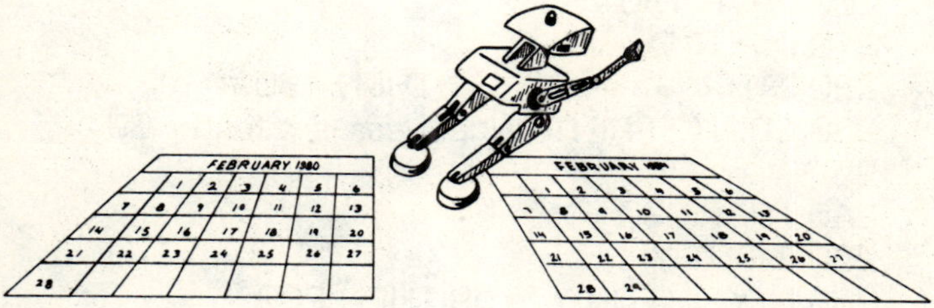

```
10 REM *** DATE CONVERTER ***
20 REM
30 REM Converts standard date format
40 REM to Julian date format.
50 REM
60 DIM M(12), D(31), Y(100), J(366)
70 DIM A$(1)
100 REM  ************
110 REM USER INPUT
120 REM  ************
130 PRINT CHR$(125)
140 PRINT ," JULIAN DATE CONVERTER"
150 PRINT : PRINT "What month is it (enter 1-12)";
160 TRAP 150
170 INPUT M
180 IF M < 1 OR M > 12 THEN 140
190 PRINT : PRINT "What day is it";
200 TRAP 190
210 INPUT D
220 IF D < 1 OR D > 31 THEN 190
230 PRINT : PRINT "What year is it (enter 00 -
99)";
240 TRAP 230
250 INPUT Y
260 IF Y < 0 OR Y > 99 THEN 230
300 REM ********************
310 REM FIND JULIAN DATE
320 REM ********************
330 ON M GOTO 340, 350, 360, 370, 380, 390,
400, 410, 420, 430, 440, 450
340 J = D : GOTO 530
350 J = 31 + D : GOTO 530
360 J = 59 + D : GOTO 530
370 J = 90 + D : GOTO 530
380 J = 120 + D : GOTO 530
390 J = 151 + D : GOTO 530
400 J = 181 + D : GOTO 530
410 J = 212 + D : GOTO 530
```

```
420 J = 243 + D : GOTO 530
430 J = 273 + D : GOTO 530
440 J = 304 + D : GOTO 530
450 J = 334 + D : GOTO 530
500 REM ***************************
510 REM CHECK FOR LEAP YEAR
520 REM ***************************
530 RESTORE
540 READ N
550 IF N = 999 THEN 630
560 IF N = Y AND M <> 1 THEN J = J + 1 :
GOTO 630
570 GOTO 540
600 REM ************************
610 REM PRINT JULIAN DATE
620 REM ************************
630 PRINT : PRINT "JULIAN DATE IS: ";
640 IF J < 10 THEN PRINT Y; "."; "00"; J : GOTO
670
650 IF J < 100 THEN PRINT Y; "."; "0"; J : GOTO
670
660 PRINT Y; "."; J
670 PRINT : PRINT "Do you wish to convert another
date"
680 PRINT "(answer Y or N)";
690 TRAP 680
700 INPUT A$
710 IF A$ = "Y" THEN 130
720 IF A$ <> "N" THEN 670
730 PRINT CHR$(125)
740 PRINT : PRINT "PROGRAM ENDED."
750 END
800 REM ********************
810 REM LEAP YEAR DATA
820 REM ********************
830 DATA 84, 88, 92, 96, 0, 999
```

Programming Notes